100 Questions from My Child

100 Questions from My Child

MALLIKA CHOPRA

Foreword by

DEEPAK CHOPRA

RODALE

Rodale books may be purchased for business or promotional use or for special sales. For information, please write to: Special Markets Department, Rodale, Inc., 733 Third Avenue, New York, NY 10017

Printed in the United States of America
Rodale Inc. makes every effort to use acid-free ♾, recycled paper ♻.

Book design by Christina Gaugler

Library of Congress Cataloging-in-Publication Data

Chopra, Mallika
    100 questions from my child / Mallika Chopra ; foreword by Deepak Chopra.
        p.   cm
    ISBN-13 978–1–59486–600–5   hardcover
    ISBN-10 1–59486–600–7   hardcover
    1. Parenting—Religious aspects.   2. Parent and child.   I. Title: II. Title: One hundred questions from my child.
    BL625.8.C65   2007
    204'.41—dc22   2007001562

Distributed to the trade by Holtzbrinck Publishers

2   4   6   8   10   9   7   5   3   1   hardcover

We inspire and enable people to improve their lives and the world around them
For more of our products visit **rodalestore.com** or call 800-848-4735

DEDICATION

I would like to express my deep gratitude to all the people in Tara and Leela's lives who take the time to patiently answer their questions. This book is dedicated to you.

To their great-grandparents, who set the example for all of us to listen to, and learn from, our children. You are eternally in our hearts.

To Nani, Nana, Dadi, Dada, Mamu, Mami, and Chachu. Tara and Leela are blessed to know a family that is truly dedicated to nurturing their bodies, minds, and souls.

To Manorama whose patience, love, and values are echoed in her very words and actions. We will be forever grateful to you and to Jenny for all you have done for our family.

To their teachers—particularly those at Circle of Children—who amaze us daily with their wisdom, laughter, and genuine passion for teaching our most precious children.

To the aunts and uncles, the cousins, the other parents, and the many friends who take the time to patiently listen to the questions—those many questions— that require thoughtful, often challenging answers.

And, last but not least, to Sumant. For whenever a question is too difficult to answer, you are always there for me to say, "Ask your father."

And he said: "I tell the truth, unless you change and become like little children, you will never enter the kingdom of heaven.

Therefore, whoever humbles himself like this child is the greatest in the kingdom of heaven."

Matthew 18: 3–4

Contents

FOREWORD

by Deepak Chopra

One of the most basic **human instincts is the desire to know. We want to** know about ourselves, **about our relationships, and about the world.**

We begin this process **as soon as we become even a little self-aware. Every** child asks the most basic existential **questions: "Where did I come from?," "What** happens to animals and people **when they die?," "How does a rainbow get its col**ors?," "Why do you love me?," **"What makes me happy?," "What makes me sad?"**

Asking a question is the **most fundamental human activity because in the asking of** the question is the key to knowledge, **understanding, intuition, imagination, creativ**ity, the power of intention, **and conscious choice making. When a child's question is** met with indifference, a child **loses her/his creativity** and becomes a victim of the hypothesis of social conditioning—**which, at best, can lead to a banal and trivial life.**

Every wisdom tradition **says, "Ask and you shall receive." Whom do you ask?** Everyone. You ask yourself, **you ask those whom you trust and admire, and ask those** who have opinions quite different **from yours. Ultimately, you take all of the answers** given to you and come up **with the deepest truth from the depth of your being.**

For a parent, nothing is **more important than encouraging your children to ask** as many questions as possible **and, in turn, to also participate in the questioning of** everything we take for granted. **At the deepest level of our being, our soul has a** knowingness of all that exists. The knowingness that results with intimacy of our soul results in spontaneous right action: the ability to make the most evolutionary choice in every situation that happens. But the soul must be nurtured through questioning. Who am I? What are my deepest desires? What is my purpose in life? What is the contribution I wish to make to the world? What are the moments of my peak experience? Who are my heroes and heroines in religion, mythology, and history? What are the qualities that I look for in a best friend? What are my unique talents? What are the best qualities that I express in my relationships? These questions shape the meanings and context of our life as we go from childhood to maturity.

When my own children (including Mallika, the author of this book) were growing up, we would often read stories, fairy tales, and mythology together. I would frequently stop reading when we came to "a cliff-hanger" and tell them to complete the story the next day by asking the right questions. It was fascinating for us to see how many versions of the same story we could create with the same cast of characters.

Our life is a story we tell ourselves. But if we don't ask questions, the story becomes predictable, banal, and ordinary. The more questions we ask, the more possibilities we see in the stories of our lives and the more freedom and creativity we find. Life becomes an adventure of mystery, magic, and enlightenment.

Today, we recognize that even science does not describe and explain nature, but nature is exposed to our method of questioning. The questions we ask change the world we see. And because human nature is a part of nature, there is nothing more important but the questions we ask of ourselves. The great Sufi poet Rumi said, "The whole universe exists inside you, ask all from yourself." The universe remains a field of possibilities until the moment we ask the question—and then, it is compelled to make a choice!

In this book, Mallika explores questions asked to her by her children. Some of the questions are very recognizable; others will take you completely by surprise because they are original and have never been asked before. In exploring these questions, a new reality awakens, and in that new reality, there is creative evolution and freedom.

The best gift you can give to your children is to encourage them to ask questions and to explore all possible answers with them; to not be attached to one version. As a parent and a grandparent, I hope you will gain as much insight into the innate genius of children and their infinite potential as I did when reading these questions and answers and engaging in conversation with my two little granddaughters.

Just like Mallika's children asked questions that evoked spontaneous feelings in Mallika, you too must encourage your children to ask these questions and more. I hope you read this book aloud to them so they, too, can start to live the questions, and one day move into the answers.

INTRODUCTION

As a mom, I realized early on that my children were looking to me for answers.

Even before they could speak, they were asking questions—questions about how to interact with the world, about what was safe, what was good or bad in their world. And it was my reaction to these questions that began to shape their worldview, their sense of security and trust.

And, of course, as Tara, my elder daughter, became more vocal, she was actually able to put her questions into words, unleashing an unending hunger for information, explanations, justifications, and confirmations. Question after question after question!

While it became exhausting to constantly answer her questions, I also saw how my answers really shaped how she reacted to things. With almost every action and word, I influenced how she processed information and reacted to everyday stimuli. Once I gave her an answer, that explanation stuck with her for a long time. When I became impatient and gave her a haphazard answer, it could take months to convince her to think another way!

There were what seemed to be the easier questions: Why do I have to eat my vegetables? Why do I have to go to bed now? Why can't I watch TV? And often, I realized even these questions were difficult, and the answers would result in tantrums and lots of distress.

But then, there were the harder ones. It was the questions like "Where is Maa?"—a question she posed to me after my grandmother died and I was upset—or, "Mommy, what's a bomb?"—which she asked after seeing a report about a terrorist attack on television—that became the ones that really challenged me.

I realized that answering these deeper questions required my own soul searching, for there were many questions I really did not know how to answer. They were questions that made me think about what I believed in and how I perceived my world. And I felt a sense of responsibility to give thoughtful answers that fostered love, confidence, and contemplation. There were also many times when I had to admit to my daughters that I really did not know how to answer a question and that it was okay not to know.

As their mother, I was creating a context for them to ask and answer questions, setting the framework for how they would approach situations, challenges, and experiences for the rest of their lives. I realized that many times my daughters came up with the answers to questions, sometimes the most difficult ones, by themselves. In fact, their answers were often much more profound than anything I could ever think of.

As I watched them discover the world and find their answers, I was often amazed at their inherent wisdom, connection, and clarity. As I continue my parenting journey, I realize that my daughters are truly also my teachers. Through our conversations, our struggles, and our laughter, I continue to learn and search and question day after day. I will forever be grateful to both of them for challenging me to continually seek and grow and love.

This book is a collection of some of the questions and answers that my daughters and my family have explored together. When Tara or Leela, my younger daughter, asks me a question with their big, curious, loving, and trusting eyes, I want more than anything else to give them answers that make sense. My hope is that even when I can't answer all their questions, I can cultivate in them a sense of self-discovery, a willingness to be open, and a desire to keep asking more questions.

ABOUT MY DAUGHTERS

I wrote this book when my elder daughter, Tara, had already turned 4 years old and my younger daughter, Leela, was approaching 2 years old.

My daughters have two very different personalities, and they each teach me in their own ways. At this stage, Tara is truly my little companion. Her maturity and wisdom and insight surprise me every day. Tara's words and questions create the framework of this book. I am sure other parents will hear the echo of their own children's wisdom in her contemplation.

And Leela is my little baby who makes me laugh and play. As she prances about the house, singing her songs, she reminds my husband (Sumant), Tara, and me that life is about love and giggles and hugs and kisses.

Who Am I?

"Mommy, if God is inside me,
why can't I feel him moving around?"

HENRY (AGE 5)

What does my name mean?

"Am I Tara?" she asked.

It was the end of a long day, and we were drawing and relaxing in the playroom. Downtime. A time when we chatted about the day before getting ready for bed, a time to connect.

"Yes, you are Tara." My precious Tara, I thought.

"What does Tara mean?"

I took her hands—my daughter's hands were long and fine. No longer baby hands, but the hands of a sophisticated 4½-year-old.

"Tara is a star, the brightest star in the universe. Did you know that the Buddha's mother's name was Tara—the compassionate one?"

"What does Leela mean?" She pointed to her younger sister.

"Leela is the play, the dance, of the universe."

"She does love to play," Tara giggled. Leela, 2 years old, pointed to herself and said, "Yaya. Yaya." (Her pronunciation of Leela.) She then did her unique dance—arms bent, shoulders bouncing up and down, head bobbing from side to side, little jumps that did not really get her off the ground.

"Why are we Tara and Leela?"

I smiled, because somehow each of them had taken on the personalities of their names.

"You are Tara because you came to our world as a star that brightened up our whole universe. You made everyone around you feel peaceful and loving. You made our hearts warm and safe." I gave her a tight hug and kissed her soft head.

I looked at my dancing toddler. "And Leela came to our world to remind us to laugh and play and dance. She stirred our hearts with her giggles and her teasing eyes."

"Dance, dance," Leela sang. "Aha! Aha! Aha!"

Tara and I looked at each other, and then laughingly mimicked her movements. The three of us danced freely in our universe of bright, giggling stars.

Question for Your Child

Do you know what your name means to me?

2

Peekaboo. Where are you?

Leela's first game was playing peekaboo. Covering her eyes, she thought no one could see her. She would put her little hands over her eyes, hold her breath, and then shriek, "Boo!" Her hands would take a few seconds to come off her eyes, and then she would giggle as she started the game again. She could play this game over and over again and never seemed to tire of it.

Big sister Tara would lead Leela behind a curtain or under the bed, and together they would call out, "I'm hiding! I'm hiding!" I'd walk around the house. "Where's Tara? Where's Leela?" Hearing the giggles, I continued to play along. I could hear 4-year-old Tara telling 1½-year-old Leela that it is important to wait. What a discovery for my little one to learn about space and patience and being quiet!

Leela would jump out. "Boo!" Later, she would say, "Mama, where are you?" Every time I was out of sight, I would hear her calling, "Wey ah u? Mama, wey ah u?"

One day, I was in the kitchen, and Leela called out for me from the playroom. She started to get frustrated when I did not answer immediately. I was about to walk into the playroom when I heard Tara telling Leela, "Leela, Mama is always here." She was pointing to Leela's heart. "You don't ever have to worry, because even if you can't see Mama, you can always feel her in your heart."

3

Am I the most beautiful girl in the world?

When Tara was young, we lauded her with loving praises. She was the smartest girl in the world. The most beautiful girl in the world. The most special girl in the whole wide world.

All was wonderful until Leela, her little sister, came along. Because now we had the two most beautiful girls, the two smartest, the two most special girls in the world. But that didn't really work.

We realized that, in our loving innocence, we had programmed her to need and want to be the best. She was very competitive and got upset if she heard someone else being praised, without the person acknowledging her as well.

One afternoon, Tara got really upset that I was praising Leela for looking beautiful in a new dress.

"But, Mama, I am the most beautiful girl in the world!" she demanded me to acknowledge. I realized it was time for a transition to a new way of thinking.

"You are beautiful, baby. But Leela is also beautiful."

"No, I am more beautiful." She was focused and determined.

"But, Mama, you said I was the most beautiful!" Her lips began to quiver, and my heart broke as I saw tears well up in her eyes.

I picked her up, hugged, and kissed her.

"Baby, you are beautiful, beautiful, beautiful! You will always be the most beautiful Tara in my world. But Leela is also beautiful. She is beautiful as Leela. And you are beautiful as Tara. Everyone is the most beautiful when they are who they are."

She listened. I continued to hug and kiss her. I felt I needed to be loving and supportive, but stay committed to this new line of thinking.

"But, Mama, I want to be the best."

"Actually, no one really has to be the best, because each one of us has our own special beauty. We should try to be happy about other people's beauty as well. When we are happy about that, then we become more beautiful."

She listened intently. This would take time, I thought. Time, attention, and lots of hugs and kisses.

4

Am I boring?

Every afternoon when I pick up Tara from school, we discuss her day. Sometimes she is chatty, and other times she tells me that she doesn't want to talk. Tara loves her school, teachers, and friends, and her mood, whether quiet or contemplative, is generally happy and fulfilled by the day.

So one afternoon when I picked her up and could sense her sadness, I wanted to find out what had happened. "Sweetie, how was your day at school?"

She was quiet. I asked again.

"Mama, my friends told me that they didn't want to play with me today because I was boring."

My heart stopped for a moment.

"And what did you say?" I asked.

"I started to cry and told them that I still wanted to play with them." And then she told me about how her teacher came and talked with Tara and her friends and told them about how words could hurt another's feelings.

Oh, how my heart was breaking! How could anyone tell my special baby that she was boring? She did not even understand what boring meant, and I am sure her friends didn't either. But all of them seemed to sense what emotions the word would create.

There was silence in the backseat as I tried to think about how to make my 4½-year-old daughter feel nurtured and safe and empowered again.

"Sweetie, you are not boring. You are smart and beautiful and creative and funny and so, so, so special!"

"I want to tell you something," I continued. "Sometimes when other people are feeling sad or angry, they say things to hurt those around them. You have to remember when they say things like 'you are boring,' it's really about them, not about you."

Tara listened quietly. And my instinct told me to shift our attention to something else. "Tara, how about you and I spend some special time together and go get an ice cream!" I saw her smile return, and she nodded her head happily.

That evening when Sumant came home and asked Tara about school, she told him about what had happened. Sumant looked at me with concern as she told her story. After she described her teacher's talk with her and her friends, she continued, "But you know, Papa, when people say things like that, it is really about them, not about me."

Sumant and I looked at each other. Had she understood what I had said? Had she internalized that? I prayed that she had, promising myself to get some advice from Tara's teacher about how to talk to her about such situations in the future.

5

Why can't I stop crying?

Most evenings, at some point or another, the Bollywood movies come on in our house. Tara dresses up in the lehngas (traditional Indian skirt and blouse) that her grandmother sends from India, and dances around, hips shaking, eyes sparkling, shoulders moving up and down. Leela tries to copy her big sister, her stout little legs bouncing up and down, her knees trying to bend, but not really.

The music makes them happy, and they express that happiness with every fiber of their being. They laugh and sing and are totally pure in their joy.

And they do this with other emotions as well—sadness, loneliness, fear, excitement. There are times when they want to cuddle, to feel and give love. They do this openly, asking for it if my attention is not fully there. And there are times when they just want to cry. Not the crying of a tantrum or a fall, but just crying because somewhere inside, they are sad, confused, hurt.

One evening when Tara's whining had gotten to me and she had started crying, I thought I could distract her with a story or a game. But she wouldn't stop, and she actually asked, "Mama, why can't I stop crying?"

I tried to probe what was bothering her. Was she missing her father, who was traveling? Was she scared of something? Did something hurt her?

"Mama, I just feel sad."

I realized that she was being true to herself. She was embracing her emotions and expressing them. There was no need to justify them.

I realized she just needed to be held and loved. She needed to feel that her tears were just as precious and pure as her laughter.

Question for Your Child

What makes you happiest?

6

Can I get rid of my shadow?

One sunny morning, when Leela was 1½ years old, she discovered her shadow. She was standing by the window and noticed the dark image on the white wall. She reached out to touch it, and in moving, saw that it moved. She moved again, and the shadow moved again. She started to giggle and wiggled from side to side.

Tara first watched her younger sister intently and after a few minutes decided to join her. Tara, hands on her hips, swayed from side to side, and Leela jumped up and down now with excitement. I put on some music, and they performed a shadow dance against the wall. I showed them with my hands how to make bunny ears and a fish.

The shadow discovery was a fun one. When we went for a walk outside, Tara and I pointed out to Leela her shadow and she reached down to touch it. She gleefully watched her shadow as she waddled down the sidewalk.

On this walk, Tara decided that she was tired of her shadow and wanted to get rid of it.

"Mama, I don't want my shadow anymore. Can you take it away?"

Leela was now trying to catch Tara's shadow in the sidewalk.

"Let's see, Baby, can you get rid of it?"

Tara jumped from side to side. She ran forward and backward. She turned around in a circle, but her shadow followed her in every direction. "I want it to go away." She was frustrated and really didn't want it anymore. "Why don't you want it anymore?" I asked.

She didn't answer. She was still trying to get rid of it.

I walked the kids under a shaded tree, and the shadow was now gone. Leela moved on to play with the grass, as Tara confirmed the shadow had gone.

"Why don't you want it anymore?" I asked again.

"I was just tired of it following me," she responded, happy to have a rest from her shadow for a while.

I pushed a bit. "I think, Tara, that your shadow is always with you. It is something that's a part of you, something special."

"Remember how Peter Pan lost his shadow?" she said. And, without his shadow, I explained, he was sad. He wanted it to be a part of him so he could be human, and Wendy sewed it back on for him.

"Sometimes, Mama, it's good to let your shadow rest so you can get more energy. I am ready to go back in the sun now."

At that point, we continued on our walk—Tara and Leela skipping down the sidewalk—as I marveled at what a deep insight Tara had just rattled off.

7

Am I Indian or American?

When Tara consciously started processing that people looked different, she became fascinated by where people came from. She would point to people on the street and label them. The game could get complicated.

"She is Chinese."

"She is Japanese, I think, but she looks like she could be from China. How do I tell the difference?"

"She is Indian, but she does look a bit like my friend from Pakistan."

"She is black—is she from America or Africa?"

"She is American, because she is white."

I corrected her. "Actually, her skin color is white, or you can say Caucasian. But she could be from the United States or some place in Europe."

And she would often ask, "Mama, am I Indian or American?"

"You are lucky, Tara!" I would explain. "You are both Indian and American. Your parents and grandparents were born in India, so you are Indian. But, since you were born and live in the United States, you are also American. I too am Indian and American."

"So, what is Mango?" Mango was one of Tara's dearest friends who was half Chinese and half Indian. "Well, Mango is also American because she lives in the United States. But she is also part Chinese and part Indian because her grandparents came from those places."

"So is your body made from a certain place?" She was trying to understand.

"Yes, I guess you could say that your body comes from the different places that your parents and grandparents came from. But then, you can live in a different place and also be from there..."

As I began to confuse myself with my own words, I realized how Tara's world was becoming more and more a world of global citizens. People from different places living in different places connecting with those from different places. It was important for me, as her mother, to inculcate a sense of connection with people, no matter what race, nationality, or religion.

"But, Tara, no matter where people are from or what they look like, all people share certain things. We all laugh and cry, feel happy or sad, love..." I continued to focus on the things we shared with other people. Tara listened for a bit and joined me in listing things that we all have in common. "Like we all love our mamas, and we all have to eat our fruits and vegetables to grow..."

I smiled at my daughter's innocent world. "Yes, eating and growing up are things we have in common with people from all around the world. And most important, everyone loves someone no matter where they come from." And so Tara and I began exploring what we shared with others and sought pride in what made us different.

8

How do I know who's in my family?

"**M**ama, why do you say your name is Mallika *Chopra*, and Papa, Leela, and I are all *Mandals*?" Tara asked.

I smiled. Using Chopra as my last name had just kind of happened. It was not a conscious choice, as such. Since Sumant was not attached to "Mandal" and for work "Chopra" seemed easier, I had just continued to use it after we got married. Once I had children, it had become more complicated. I often felt a need to clarify that I was their mother or stress that their father and I were still married. In fact, for school and for doctor's appointments, I often would use "Mandal."

I looked at Tara. "Sweetie, usually when children are born, they take their father's last name. Also, usually when a girl gets married, she takes her husband's last name. But if she wants, she can keep her old name." Articulating the process made it seem all the more random to me.

Tara interjected, "But, what does a last name mean?"

"A name is just a way that we label ourselves. It helps us to organize people in our lives, remind us who is in our family, in our friends' families…"

"So are you part of Nani and Nana's family, and Leela and I are part of Papa's family? Why aren't you part of our family, Mama?" Her question was totally genuine.

"My darling. I am totally part of our family. Our family is you, Papa, Leela, and me. But it is also my parents, Papa's parents, and our brothers and sisters, our grandparents, cousins, aunts, uncles. We are all part of one family, whether we are Chopras or Mandals. When Papa and I got married, we connected our families!"

"So getting married is connecting families?" Tara, at 4½, had a fascination with marriage. This seemed like a cool concept.

"Yes, and every time someone in our family gets married, then we get a bigger family! Since Gautam (my brother) married Candice, we can think of her family as part of ours as well."

Tara thought for a moment and laughed. "We have Chinese family members, as well? Because, Candice is a Chen…"

That's right, I smiled. "Our family keeps getting bigger and bigger! Aren't we lucky?"

I saw that Tara was still trying to resolve something in her mind. "So, whether you are a Chopra or a Mandal doesn't matter, because now Chopra and Mandals are all together."

"Absolutely," I agreed. Tara reminded me that ultimately our labels connected us and that was all that really mattered.

Question for Your Child

Who is in our family?

9

Where was I at your wedding?

One of our favorite activities to do as a family is to look through old photographs. I like to show Tara and Leela pictures of their great grandparents, grandparents, cousins, aunts, and uncles. They point to familiar faces and ask about ones that they don't recognize.

One set of photographs that they both love to look at is our wedding pictures. Their eyes open wide and sparkle as they look at the colorful, rich outfits and beautiful jewelry. They love the fact that Mama looks like a real princess.

Every time we look at the wedding photographs, Tara asks me the same question.

"But, Mama, where was I at your wedding?" Then before I can answer, she smiles and answers, "I was waiting in your tummy!"

And we talk about how she decided to come into the world as the perfect present for Mama and Papa and all her family. And how Leela waited for the perfect time to bless us once again. In this way, we begin exploring the nature of our souls, and how our existence is not bound by space and time.

Tara once told me a story about where she was before she came out of Mama's tummy—a princess in Alaska taking care of penguins. After the penguins got married, she decided it was time to come home to Mama and Papa.

10

Will I be different when I am 27 years old?

One day, Tara became fascinated by the concept of age. She wanted to know how old everyone in the family was and wanted to list everyone that she knew in chronological order.

She was very specific that she was older than her friend, because she was $4\frac{1}{2}$ years old and her friend was just turning 4. She understood that Leela was *almost* 2. She had a bit of a challenge accepting that her baby cousin was 9 months old, because Tara was older than her cousin, and 9 was a bigger number than 4. She wanted to know what it meant to be 0.

Once we had the spectrum of ages ranked, Tara asked, "When I grow older, like when I am 27 years old, will I be different?"

"Well, you will be taller for sure! I think you are going to be much taller than Mama!" I admitted.

"And, maybe you will look different. I wonder if you will still have long hair?" I asked.

"Mama, I will always have long hair, because princesses have long hair." Of course, I nodded.

"And maybe your voice will change a bit, and your face will be bigger..."

She opened her mouth wide and stretched her face.

"But, when you are 27 years old, Tara, you will still be you! Your body will change, you may think differently about some things—like princesses—but inside you will be the same. You will be the same Tara."

She laughed and playfully nodded her head. "And, Mama, don't worry." She nodded her head teasingly. "I know, I know. I will still be your baby—even when I am 27 years old!"

How Does
My Body Work?

"When you're dead, can I see your bones?"

CHARLIE (AGE 3)

11

Why won't my princess shoes fit me anymore?

Tara had a favorite pair of princess shoes. Sparkling red shoes that were full of red glitter. When she wore these shoes, she danced and twirled. Just wearing them made her smile—she felt pretty and special and happy.

One day, however, the shoes did not fit her anymore. She had been struggling for several weeks to get them on—first wearing thinner socks, and then wearing no socks at all. Finally, the moment came when she had to admit that they were too small for her. "Why won't my princess shoes fit me anymore?" she asked, her eyes sad and sullen.

"Because you are growing up!" I smiled.

"How will I be a princess if I can't wear my princess shoes? Why do I have to grow?"

I realized my initial response had not set the right tone for the moment. If growing up meant letting go of her favorite princess shoes, I imagine she would resent it. I thought of another analogy. "Remember how we planted some sunflower seeds several months ago?"

She nodded, probably wondering what this had to do with her sparkly shoes.

"And remember how we had to water the plants so that they would grow?"

She smiled. She had loved using her pink gardening pitcher to water the plants every day. She had not known what was going to grow, or when or how, but the process had been fun.

"And do you remember how excited we were when we saw the first part of the stem come out of the soil? And how it grew and grew into a beautiful sunflower!"

"Mom, not one flower! There were six flowers!" she corrected me.

"So, in the same way that the flower grew from a seed, you are growing. And every day you are becoming bigger and taller and more beautiful, just like the flower."

She paused. "But aren't I beautiful now?"

I smiled. There was a leap in my logic that didn't make sense. Leave it to Tara to catch that!

"Of course you are beautiful now. You are my beautiful princess!" This brought us back to the shoes.

Her eyes welled with tears. "But Mom, if I grow up, I won't be able to be a princess anymore."

I took her in my arms and told her she would always be a princess, whether she had sparkly shoes or not. And then I made her a special offer.

"How about we go to the shoe store and see if they have a pair of sparkly princess shoes, but for a bigger girl?" As quickly as the tears had come, now a smile beamed across her face.

"But maybe this time, we can get pink princess shoes instead of red ones. Now that I am a big girl, my favorite color is pink."

Why don't girls have those tails like boys do?

This question seems to take many forms, but at some stage most children start to wonder about the human body. And, in particular, why are boys and girls made different?

A friend's daughter, Genevieve, was 2 years old when she asked her father, "Daddy, is your lala (vagina) broken?"

There are the questions about sitting versus standing. Why do girls always sit, but boys sit and stand? How do boys decide if they are going to sit or stand?

For Tara, she wondered why Papa had a tail and we girls did not. And she giggled when she observed, "And Mommy, his tail is in the front, not the back!"

Early on, answering the boys versus girls question didn't seem so difficult—I just stated that boys and girls were made different.

And when, at 3 years old, she asked, "But, Mommy, *why* are boys and girls made different?" I instinctively answered, "Because nature decided to make both boys and girls to keep life interesting." I wasn't ready as yet to explain the mechanics of how we used those parts differently, and it didn't seem that Tara needed to know just then.

But, in the back of my mind, I knew the questions about sex would be coming, probably sooner than I wanted to admit. As I thought about how to one day discuss sex with my daughters, I made a commitment to be honest and give appropriate information. Sex encompassed biological functions—different bodies, how we make babies—but also emotional ones that were important to discuss. Talking about how boys and girls are different was a first and good step. In my heart, I knew that if I proceeded with openness and trust, listening to the progression of my daughter's maturity and questions, our conversations about sex would only bring us closer.

13

Did you forget your eyes?

My eyesight is weak. I wear contacts, and my world is very fuzzy without them. At night, I put on my glasses, just to read before sleeping.

We were on a family holiday and one contact ripped. I did not have an extra pair. For 4 days, I wore only my crooked glasses that had a lower prescription, and my world literally looked and felt different. And the first one to sense it was my daughter Tara. "Mama, how come you aren't wearing your eyes?" she asked.

I playfully referred to my contacts as *my eyes,* and Tara had taken this literally. I explained how my contacts, not my eyes, had ripped, and I needed my glasses to see.

"How come you have to wear those to see? I don't have to wear eyes."

I smiled. Different eyes see differently. My eyes needed some help to see, so I used contacts. Did you know that dogs see differently from us, as do elephants and chameleons? Different people, different animals, all see differently.

"So, if dogs wear glasses, will they see like you and me?" Good question, I thought.

"Well, I don't know any dogs who wear glasses!" I laughed. "But if dogs did wear glasses, it would help them see the world and to do what they needed to do."

Tara took my hand. "Don't worry, Mama, I did not forget my eyes. I will make sure you see what you need to see."

14

How did I get Papa's legs?

Tara has very long legs. We play a game in which I tickle her and say, "Your legs are never-ending! They just keep going and going and going!" She stretches her legs out long and shows them off to me.

People will notice how tall she is and say to her, "Your legs are just like your daddy's! You are going to be a tall girl!" And Tara smiles.

One day, she wanted to know why she had Papa's legs and not Mama's. (Sumant is very tall with long legs. Alas, I am not so tall and do not have long legs!)

"Well," I explained, "all children are made up of parts of their mama and papa. You are a combination of us. And I am a combination of my mama and papa."

I could see Tara processing the information. I continued, "So, you have Papa's legs, but I think you have Mama's eyes." She opened her eyes wide.

"And whose neck do I have?" she asked. I tickled her neck. "Mama's neck!"

"And whose chin do I have?" This was becoming a fun game.

"Hmm. I think your chin comes from Dadi's family?" Tara called Sumant's mother "Dadi." Her side of the family had distinctive chins.

"But Papa doesn't have the same chin? And neither does Dadi?" She was perplexed.

"I know, but your cousin has the same chin, and so does Dadi's sister! See, you have parts of all of your family in your body."

"Does Leela also have your eyes, Papa's legs, and my chin?"

"Let's see." We called Leela, who was immersed in a game of blocks, over to us. She waddled happily over.

"Leela, can we see your eyes?" Leela pointed to her eyes and said, "Eyes!"

"Tara, whose eyes does Leela have?" Tara examined Leela's eyes. "I think, Mama, that she has your eyes, just like me!" I agreed.

"And, Leela, can we see your hair?" Leela proudly pointed to her head and said, "Hair!"

"Tara, did you know that Leela's hair is just like Maa's was—curly and fine." Maa was my grandmother. Tara nodded seriously.

"Leela, can we see your nose?" Leela pointed to her nose. "Nosee!"

And with that we continued our game, seeing how we were connected to each other.

15

Why can't I have milk from your tummy?

"Is she drinking milk from your tummy again?" Tara asked playfully as she watched me breastfeed Leela. In the beginning, she was totally fascinated by the entire process and concept that Leela would actually get milk from my body.

"Does your tummy make milk?" She would stand beside me as I held Leela and watch with furrowed brows. "Can I give her milk from my tummy?"

I would explain to her that when mothers had babies, they made milk that was just right for the little babies. And the babies drank this milk until they were ready to eat and drink other things.

It was interesting to me that Tara had never questioned why she couldn't have milk from my tummy anymore.

Sure enough, the next day as I was cuddling, stroking, and kissing Leela during her feed, Tara abruptly asked, "Mommy, why can't I have milk from your tummy as well?"

I had been so lost in my moment with Leela that I was startled. But looking at Tara's face, I realized that she felt like she was being left out of something very special.

I patted to a spot on the sofa next to me. "Come sit here, my darling baby!"

She came, shy and a bit resistant.

"You are such a big girl now that you don't need my milk anymore. I think you like things like pizza and chicken nuggets and ice cream better, don't you?"

She giggled a bit. "Yeah! Especially ice cream!"

I finished Leela's feed and put her down in her bassinet.

I picked up Tara and stroked and kissed her. "But just because you don't get your milk from me doesn't mean we can't hug and cuddle anymore! Come here, you!"

I picked her up in my arms and swung her around, kissing her over and over again.

Question for Your Child

What was your favorite part about being a baby?

16

Why are you spreading your germs all over me?

I pulled Tara into a big hug and was giving her kisses all over her face. We cuddled like this every day. But, today, she pushed me away.

"Mama, don't kiss me! Your germs are getting all over me, and I am going to get sick!"

The flu had been going around at school. Leela had a runny nose and cough. Tara, who followed instructions very well, was diligent about washing her hands and brushing her teeth. When Leela sneezed, she told her to use her tissue and to cover her mouth. Tara had understood her lesson on how germs spread, and was taking it seriously.

"Sweetie, well right now I don't have any bad germs, so if we cuddle, you will be okay," I pleaded. I wanted to cuddle.

"No, Mama. We can't see germs and they always spread." She recited her lesson. "So we don't know if you are giving the bad germs to me. I really don't want to get sick. I have Share Day in school tomorrow." Share Day was one of her favorite activities in school.

She was right. How did I know that I wasn't giving her the bad germs?

"But, can I ever kiss you again?" I asked.

She thought about it for a second.

"Well, maybe you can give me a light kiss on the cheek now, and I can then wash my face. And when the cold leaves Leela and my friends at school, then we can start cuddling again."

Why can't I have more candy?

There comes a point in our household when receiving a special treat becomes an expectation and a right, rather than a surprise or a reward for good behavior. Resetting the parameters is a challenging process.

"I can just have another candy right now and not one tomorrow!" Tara was yelling at me, the tears running down her face. I had given her a lollipop the day before when we came home from school—for no particular reason, just thought it would be a nice treat. But now, today, she wanted another one. She was not asking for one, not requesting one. She was screaming at the top of her lungs, throwing a tantrum of the first order.

"It's not a choice, Mama. I want the lollipop now!" Of course, there was no way I could give in now. I told her to take some time and settle down. The tantrum was in high gear and she was screaming. It was no longer about the candy. It was about getting her way.

"Tara, I am going to go to the other room, and I need you to take some time to breathe deeply and relax. When I come back, we can talk about this."

I left the room and she shouted, "I WANT MY CANDY!"

It took 10 minutes until the ranting and raving stopped, and I re-entered the room.

"Okay, can we talk now? How can I give you what you want if I can't even understand what you are saying because you are screaming so much?"

The tears rolled down her face, and she stated, "I want my candy."

We went through the routine conversation: What happens to your teeth if you have too much candy? Didn't the doctor say only one sweet a day? What happens if we have too much sugar?

But no matter what angle I tried, it always came back to wanting and needing her candy. And I could see that the tantrum was about to erupt again.

Finally, I decided it was enough discussion. "Tara, I am not going to give you any candy right now. We are going to set a rule that if you eat all your vegetables at lunch and dinner, then you can have something sweet. Maybe delicious fruit or yogurt, sometimes ice cream, perhaps a bite of chocolate."

The tears were coming again, and I knew we were in for a difficult night.

These were the moments that being a parent challenged me. It would take so little to make her stop crying—really, what was the big deal in giving her one small candy? But I knew that without setting boundaries, at some level, I was failing both her and me. Being a mom was about teaching my children about limits and respect and how to deal with not always getting what you want. Being a mom was not just about lots of hugs and kisses, but also about saying no and waiting until the tears stop flowing.

Mommy, why can't you take my pain away?

There are certain moments that are unbearable when you are a mother. One night when she was a baby, Leela woke up screaming and squirming in intense gas pain. It was a cry that I had never heard from her, a cry that scared me at my core. I tried to hold and comfort her, but she writhed her body in every direction, and I was scared I would actually drop her. I still tried to hold her tight, to sing to her, to rock her back and forth, but she couldn't be consoled.

Her eyes looked at me, pleading. I knew she was begging me, "Mommy, take the pain away! Mommy, please take the pain away." And I could do nothing to help.

Nothing, but be there for her.

I realized in that moment the heartache that parents go through when their children are in deeper pain—what helplessness actually feels like, what frustration means at its very core. That there are certain things that are truly beyond our control, and that we must reach a place of acceptance where we have to let our children experience what they are meant to experience.

And that there are times when we really cannot do anything except love with all our hearts. We will be there to hold their hands, to hug them, to give them a million kisses.

How do bodies get better?

My brother, whom Tara and Leela call Gotham Mamo, was having knee surgery. It was a standard, planned ACL procedure, and among my family we were planning logistics to help him through his recovery.

The day before the surgery, Tara came to me, her lip quivering, tears forming in her eyes, and asked, "Mama, is Gotham Mamo going to die tomorrow?" As she uttered these words, my 4-year-old baby broke down, the tears flowing down from her big, innocent eyes.

"No, baby, no." I held her close.

"Then why is he going to the hospital? Why is he going to the doctor?"

The fear was so raw, so deep, so touching. I hugged her and explained that the doctor was going to help him feel stronger, that the doctor was going to fix his broken knee. We talked about how the doctor had taken Leela out of Mama's tummy and that was a good, happy thing.

Only later did I start to process her questioning and think about how she had created the association between the surgery, doctor, sickness, and death. My grandmother had recently died, and Tara had been witness to many conversations about her sickness. My cousin had gone through chemotherapy, and lost his sight and hearing, while Tara was between 2 and 3 years old. These fears had been quietly building up inside her.

"I think, Mama, that we should make a card for him so that he feels good and knows we love him."

"Good idea," I told her. "And we should then take the card and give it to him, so that you can give him a kiss as well." A big smile spread across her face.

It was important to show Tara, not just tell her, that Gotham was going to be just fine. After his surgery, we consciously spent more time at his house. She was able to see him struggle at first with the pain and then get better and stronger day by day. We talked about how the doctor was helping him and showed her the medicines he was taking that helped take the pain away. After a few days, we pointed out that the pain was now going away by itself.

Through participating in his healing process, Tara was able to perceive that many challenges can be overcome.

20

When you get old, will you get sick and die?

My grandmother, Maa, was a loving, compassionate, strong woman. She had a presence that often dominated a room. She had opinions. She was a negotiator. She ruled her family and community. She loved aggressively. She took care of people. She was involved in everything, and the world seemed to revolve around her. In many ways, Maa had a larger-than-life personality.

It was very important to me that Maa got to know my children. But by the time I had Tara, Maa was very sick and weak. She lay in bed most of the day, and it was extremely painful for her to get up and sit in a chair. But during my visits to India, she would get out of bed and come to the living room. She would sit in her chair and watch Tara as she played or ate or crawled about. She could hardly speak, and I would have to sit very close to her to hear her words. Her mind was as sharp as ever, and in her whispers was specific advice on how to deal with my latest parenting struggle.

During a visit to India when Tara was just over 3 years old, Tara began to observe Maa more carefully during our visits. I had shown Tara pictures of Maa and Daddy (my grandfather who had passed away before Tara was born) in which Maa was vibrant and beautiful and strong. But when Tara actually saw Maa, she was skin and bones, was weak, and could hardly speak. Tara would ask me, "Why does she look like a boy?" (Maa's hair was cut short now.) and "Why does she sleep all day long?" (At that stage, we would go and sit in bed with Maa.) Tara would cling to me and say, "I am scared of her." It made me want to cry, because, to me, Maa was everything other than what Tara saw.

"No, sweetie. Maa is just old and she is sick. She is my grandmother, and I love her like you love your Nani and Dadi (her two grandmothers)."

Maa died soon after that trip to India. Tara understood that I was upset, and she would cuddle with me without saying anything. I would tell Tara that finally Maa could rest in peace, that she was no longer sick and tired, and she was with Daddy.

More than 6 months after Maa died, Tara asked me one day, "Mama, when you get old, will you also get sick and die? Is my grandmother going to get sick and die also?" The question was totally out of the blue. But in it, I heard the echo of my own anguish about what Maa had gone through in her last years of life. I heard my own fears about how a woman who represented strength and life to me had become so weak. And I faced my own denial that such a fate could happen to me.

I sat down and put Tara in my lap. "Well, as we get older, we get wiser. Do you know that Maa used to give me hints about how to make your tummy better and how to help you sleep at night?" Tara listened intently.

"I hope that as I get older, I will be as wise as Maa. And just because I get older, it doesn't mean I will also get sick!" I smiled to lighten the mood as I spoke.

"But, will you die?" It was a direct question.

"Sweetie, when it is time for me to die, yes, I will die. But I think that is a long, long, long time from now." I held her close.

"But just because we die doesn't mean we are gone," I continued. "I think about Maa all the time and tell you stories about her. So, really, she is still with me."

Tara was quiet, processing. We sat holding each other. She seemed to understand that there was nothing more to say.

Where Do I Live?

"What does light taste like?"

PATRICK (AGE 4)

21

Where does the rain come from?

One morning, it was pouring outside. Tara had just woken up and was lying in bed, gazing out the window. Leela was putting her nose against the cold glass and pointing outside while singing "Water, Water!" Because we live in Los Angeles, rain is such a treat and a nice change from sunny days. I could see how much both the girls were enjoying watching and listening to the rain on this lazy morning.

I said to Tara, "I wonder where the rain comes from."

Tara told me it comes from the clouds. Those big clouds that are in the sky.

I continued my line of questioning. "How do the clouds decide to let the rain fall?"

Tara continued to gaze, almost dreamlike, outside the window. "Mommy, when their tummies get full, they decide to let the rain go. That way, they can stay comfortable."

Leela continued to sing, and Tara formulated her story.

"And then they get hungry again. So they eat more water."

It was a perfect explanation.

Question for Your Child

What does the rain sound like to you?

22

Where does the sun go at night?

Sometimes, the way in which a question is answered is more memorable than the facts or explanation itself.

My father remembers how his uncle answered his question—where does the sun go at night?—for him when he was 5 years old. Rattan Uncle gave him a big smile and said, "Let me show you something."

Rattan Uncle took a flashlight and an orange. He told my father that the flashlight was the sun that gives light, and the orange was the Earth where we live. He marked a spot on the orange and turned off the lights in the room. He pointed the flashlight to the spot on the orange and demonstrated how half of the orange had light on it, and the other half was dark. And he began to turn the orange. My father saw how the spot now moved into darkness. "Deepak," Rattan Uncle said, "the sun is always there. It doesn't go anywhere at night. We just don't face it all the time."

My father recollects that this simple demonstration not only clearly answered his question, but the memory of the interaction warms his heart whenever he thinks about it. Rattan Uncle's loving patience and attention have stayed with my father his entire life and have served as the example for how my father now interacts with his grandchildren.

23

Where did the snowman go?

As a young girl growing up in Boston, I loved the snow. I watched the snow-flakes fall from the sky with wonder, a sprinkling of unique and delicate designs dancing in the wind. Looking up high into the clouds, I loved the tickling sensation as the snow touched my skin and turned into a drop of water.

I remember my mother bundling me up in so many clothes that it was difficult for me to walk. I clearly remember feeling the new sensation of falling as my little feet dug into the snow.

I must have been 4 years old when I joined some older friends at the park to build a snowman for the first time. I helped roll the snow, watching with amaze-ment as the small ball became larger and larger. Soon, we had three big balls piled on top of each other, and my friends were decorating the snowman with sticks for arms, rocks for eyes and nose, and leaves to decorate.

I could not stop staring at the snowman. I was so proud of our creation. Before we left the park, I asked my mother if I could put my hat on him so that he could stay warm. My mother agreed.

For the next few days, I pleaded with my mother every morning to take me to the park to go visit him. I would patch up any spots on his body.

And then one night, it rained. The next morning, when we reached the park, the snowman was gone. I was devastated.

"Where did the snowman go?" I desperately asked my mother.

My mother paused for a moment. Now, thinking back on it, I realize she was considering how to answer my question. I am so glad she answered it the way she did, because her words planted a belief in me that our souls can always return.

"Every year, when it is cold and the snow comes, the snowmen come to play and laugh with us. But they need to be in the cold to stay healthy, so when it starts to get warm, they decide to go on vacation to a place where there is still snow."

I was genuinely devastated. "But I will never see him again. I miss him."

"That is the wonderful thing about snowmen, baby." My mother's warm voice reassured me. "See, snowmen always come back, every year. They are brought back to life by the laughter and games of children."

"You mean we will get to make him again next year!" I remembered the fun I had with all the children in the park. I remembered giving him my hat and my feeling of love and pride when I saw him. I smiled at the memory.

As we walked away, I had a last thought. "Mom, where did his hat go?" We looked back at where he had stood, and there was no hat in sight.

My mother's eyes twinkled, "Well, surely he had to take it with him to keep his head warm!" I held my mother's hand tightly as I dreamt about what hat to give him next year.

24

How long is an hour?

I told Tara one Monday morning that a friend of hers was coming to visit us on the weekend.

Tara's eyes were wide with excitement. "Really, Mama! I am so so so excited!"

So began days of waiting for her friend to arrive. Every day, she would wake up and ask, "Is she coming today?" And every day, I would have to tell her that today was not the day, but she was coming soon.

"But, Mama, how long is a day?" she asked, exasperated and frustrated about waiting.

I remembered when Tara's friend, Shiva, was told that his grandparents were coming to visit. Shiva diligently went to the door to wait for them, but the problem was that they were not coming for another month! He could not grasp this concept and insisted on sleeping by the door that night.

"Well, a day is the time from when the sun comes up, goes down, and comes up again. It's going to take 4 more days before your friend comes," I tried to explain.

"Mama, is a day a lot of hours?"

"Yes, it is 24 hours."

"But how long is an hour?"

I began to explain the number of minutes, the number of seconds, and started counting.

"So, I have to wait all those seconds and minutes and hours and days before she comes!" Tara did not look happy.

Children truly live life in the moment. When they are hungry, they want food. When they are happy, they smile and laugh. When they are frustrated, they cry. Where does the process of anticipation and living for another moment in time creep in?

I changed tactics.

"An hour, Tara, aside from being lots of minutes and seconds, is a special time when we can love each other and laugh and play and dance and sing." I reached over and pulled her in my arms and tickled her, both of us giggling away.

"There are lots and lots of fun things we are going to do before your friend gets here!"

Question for Your Child

What does a second feel like?

25

Do trees have feelings?

I love to ask Tara questions and watch her face as she animatedly creates a story and tells me how the world works.

We have a beautiful tree in our front yard. I asked Tara, "Do trees have feelings?"

"Of course they do. They feel sad and happy." I realized by the shrug of her shoulders that it wasn't a provoking question. Why would the tree not have feelings?

"And, you know Mama," she continued, "when it is hot outside, the trees, they sweat like crazy!" I smiled. It was a hot day.

"If we hug a tree," I asked, "does the tree become happy?"

Tara put her arms out. Her smile said it all. The tree definitely could feel such innocent love.

"Did you know, Mama, that the tree's branches are its arms? And, with its arm it hugs the air and the sky and the birds?" Her face was full of expression, her body reaching out into the world, her soul pure. It was a beautiful image.

"Mama, it's not nice to ever hit the tree." She mimicked hitting and then shook her head. "Because the tree would feel it. It would hurt, but it also would be sad."

"So, we have to be careful to always take care of trees, don't we?" I asked.

She nodded her head and mimicked stroking the tree. I could see her mind churning, thinking about how she could take care of it. And, for a moment, I knew that the tree was listening to her thoughts, and they were connected.

Question for Your Child

Would you like to go and hug a tree with me?

26

Why are you so scared of mice?

Tara and Leela were sitting in the car when Leela, 2 years old, started screaming and shaking wildly. I looked in my rearview mirror and saw her head flailing from side to side. I quickly pulled over to the side of the road and went to see what was wrong.

Buzzing around Leela's head was a tiny little fly—it was so small you could hardly see it. But Leela was completely freaked out, and I had to take her out of her car seat to calm her down. I had never seen her so scared before.

It took a few minutes for her to stop screaming, and then we got the fly out of the car. "Shoo fly!" I waved my hands. "See, Leela, it's just a fly. Say, 'Shoo fly!'" Leela waved her arms and repeated, "Shoo fly!"

"See Baby, it's not a big deal! There's nothing to be scared about. The fly is gone." Leela continued to say, "Shoo fly! Shoo fly! All gone."

I put her back in the car and continued on our journey. "See Leela, the fly is gone. You don't have to be scared of the fly." She had settled down.

Tara now piped up. "Mama, Leela is scared of flies."

"I know, she got scared, huh? But flies are so tiny, Leela, you don't have to be scared of them!" Leela waved her hands, "Shoo fly!"

"Mama," Tara began, "why are you so scared of mice? They are small as well."

I looked back at Tara through the rearview mirror. She was right. My fear of rodents was inexplicable. It was a gut fear and even the thought of them gave me the shivers. I completely freaked out if I saw one. All my notions of not wanting to influence such a fear in my children were useless if I actually saw a rodent. It was an innate fear I could not control.

"It is true, Baby. I am scared of mice, even though they can be small." In my mind, I saw a huge rat with a long tail. Shivers ran up my spine. "But I don't think I really need to be scared of them."

"Yes, hamsters are cute. If you get to know them, you will like them," Tara stated.

Personally, even hamsters freaked me out. "Yes, hamsters can be cute," I whimpered.

"Maybe we can introduce Leela to some bugs in our garden and see if she likes them?" I asked. Tara nodded her head.

And Leela continued to wave her hands, "Shoo fly! Shoo fly!"

Question for Your Child

Is there a way to be brave even when we are scared?

27

What happened to the goldfish?

In our backyard, we have a small fountain and pond. When we moved in, the previous residents had six goldfish in the pond. Tara loved the goldfish, and whenever friends would come over to play, the first thing she would do was take them outside to feed her fish.

One morning, about 6 months after we moved in, Tara and I went to feed the goldfish and they were all gone. I could see raccoon footprints on the side of the pond and knew the raccoon had eaten up the fish.

Tara looked in the pond and, not seeing her fish, began to panic. "Mama, where are the goldfish?" She was almost 3½ years old.

How do I explain death to her, I thought? I had never thought about how to do this before, and now I started to panic. I did not want to upset her. I did not want to scar her, to make her feel insecure, helpless, scared. I wanted her to remain pure, innocent, and hopeful. I didn't want her to imagine a raccoon gobbling up her precious fish.

Her big brown eyes stared at me, waiting for an answer. And I decided to tell her the truth.

"Tara, it seems that a raccoon came, found the fish, and ate them up," I said a bit hesitantly. Her brows curled a bit, but she was listening intently.

Now I spoke with more confidence. "You see, Baby, the raccoon needs food to live, and for the raccoon, fish are a type of food."

"Oh," she said, and I could see her processing the information. "So, are the fish in the raccoon's tummy now?"

I waited for some dramatic moment, but instead she said calmly, "Mom, I love those fish. I am sad they are gone." Surprisingly, there were no tears. "I will miss them."

"Maybe we can get some new fish?" I offered.

And she smiled. "Yes, we can get new fish and tell them about the old ones. But, you know what, Mom, we should make sure we tell that raccoon to stay away this time."

"Definitely," I replied, giving her a hug now and thinking about how we could keep the raccoon away.

It took me a moment to realize how she had been so accepting about what had happened. And, once again, I thought about how important it is to speak to our children from the heart, and trust that they will be able to figure things out.

28

Are we going to disappear like the dinosaurs did?

Tara has a fascination with dinosaurs. At one point, she wanted to understand why they disappeared. I explained that different people had different ideas about what happened—perhaps the weather changed and it got too cold for them to survive, or there could have been a hot shower of stars on the planet that they did not survive. It could have been that they were getting too big and could not run fast enough to escape a predator or that they had eaten up all the plants on the earth and they had no more food.

Inevitably, the next question was, "Are we going to disappear like the dinosaurs did?" In a desire to be truthful, I told her that I didn't think anything was going to happen like that to us. But I then pushed our conversation to the next level.

I explained to her how we lived on a planet that provided us with water, food, and the right environment to survive. So, for us to live for a long, long time, we had to make sure that we didn't let the air get too hot, that we didn't pollute the waters, and that we took care of the earth.

Tara listened intently. "But, Mom, is anything going to happen to us now?"

"Darling, I don't think anything is going to happen now. But, you know what, since I love you, I have to think about what will happen in the future when you grow up! I need to make sure your world is healthy."

Tara smiled.

"And, Mama, I need to make sure it is healthy for my children, too!" Tara smiled. She loved to imagine being a mother.

As she patted her tummy and moved on to a reverie about what she would name her daughters, I felt the urgency to nurture the earth for the children that were yet to come.

Question for Your Child _____

How can we make sure the earth is healthy?

_____

29

Are there children living in space?

Looking out into space somehow connects me to spirit—the black skies that never end, the infinite stars that shimmer in the night, the peace and serenity that mask constant motion.

I love to look up into the skies with Tara and Leela. As we play games to find the moon, and count the never-ending stars, I feel that we are sharing a connection to our universe and infinity.

We will choose one star and imagine all the planets surrounding it. Tara will make up names for them and then describe what sort of life is on them. For a 4½-year-old child, each planet holds the potential for many new friends and games and places to visit.

One day, Tara got a little more contemplative while looking at the skies. "Mom, are there children living in space, for real?" Lately, she had been seeking clarification on what was real and what was imagination. "For real" had become the predominant phrase in our house.

I paused for a moment. "Actually, Tara, no one really knows if there are children on other planets. In fact, we do not know if there are even animals or other forms of life."

"Like aliens?" she asked.

I smiled. "Where did you learn about aliens?"

"My friend at school told me about them—that they have big eyes, and long necks and weird bodies. But she said they were nice if you got to know them." Someone just saw the movie *E.T.,* I thought.

"Well, I have never met an alien, and I don't know anyone who has. But I do wonder if they exist or not, and what they would be like. Sometimes, I wonder if they are looking into the skies and wondering the same things that we are."

This concept fascinated Tara, and I could see her imagination opening up to a whole new world.

We continued looking up into the skies, marveling at the secrets that lay beyond.

30

How can I take care of Mother Earth?

Think of the universe as you think of yourself.

The earth is like your body.

The air is like your breath.

The trees are like your lungs, breathing in and out the air.

The streams and rivers are like the blood circulating in your body.

And, just as you move, the earth spins in outer space, creating energy and movement.

So, as you hope to take care of yourself, take care of Mother Earth.

Let the forests and jungles thrive so that her lungs remain strong.

Plant new trees so that she can grow and thrive.

Keep the waters clean so that her blood remains fresh and healthy.

Do not pollute her soil with trash and poisons that would hurt her.

And, by taking care of Mother Earth, in turn, you will take care of yourself and those you love.

You will help her feel alive and happy so that you too can play and run and laugh in fields of colorful flowers by streams of fresh water under blue skies with bright rainbows.

How Am I Connected to Others?

"Why do I have to wear clothes?"

Sien (age 4)

31

Who is your Prince Charming?

Tara, at 3 years old, became a full-blown princess. She needed long hair, so no more haircuts. She wanted to have her toenails polished in a bright red color. She could wear only dresses (long dresses), because only dresses twirl. Even her body posture expressed her royal stature—she sat up tall, legs crossed, hands in her lap.

One evening, as Tara and I were cuddling in bed, she asked me, "Mommy, who is your Prince Charming?"

"Papa," I replied.

"No, Mommy, Papa is my Prince Charming. He cannot be yours."

And it dawned on me that in her sweet little magical world of princes and princesses, Prince Charming for Tara was always the father. Because she loved her papa most in the world, and he took care of her and made her feel secure and special.

"Well, if Papa is your Prince Charming, then who is mine?" I asked.

"Nana," she responded without hesitation. (Nana is what she calls my father.)

"Hmm. Then who is Nani's Prince Charming?" (Nani is what she calls my mother.)

"Nani," she replied. "She is just the queen."

And with that, she snuggled up in bed and drifted off into a fairyland of princess dreams.

32

Can my baby sister go away now?

When I was pregnant with Leela, Sumant and I spent a lot of time talking to Tara about the new baby who was going to join our family. Tara, who was 2½ when Leela was born, enjoyed feeling the baby's kicks in my big tummy, and she helped us choose the name, Leela.

There was so much anticipation to Leela's arrival that Tara's first meeting with Leela was an emotional one. We had kept Tara's routine as normal as possible, but the reality was that my trip to the hospital was the first time I had actually left Tara. So the context itself created some uncertainty—why did Mama have to go away?

When she came to the hospital, Sumant took Tara to the nursery to show her her baby sister. Sumant then asked her if she would like to bring the baby to Mama's room. Tara walked in, pushing the bassinet with Sumant, her face beaming with pride. "Mama, this is my baby sister! This is Leela!" I picked up Tara and smothered her with hugs and kisses! My parents, brother, and sister-in-law also peeked in the bassinet at Tara's baby.

There was absolute silence as we all watched Tara get down from my lap and look at her sister closely for the first time. Leela's eyes were open, gazing wide at her big sister. We all breathed a sigh of relief and smiled at each other. How easy was that!

The next moment, however, Tara had tears streaming down her face. She jumped back into my lap and started howling. I held her tight, asking her what had happened. It took a few minutes for me to get her to stop crying and tell me what had happened.

"Mama, I feel shy of my baby sister."

So sweetly, my daughter was trying to express all the emotion inside her—the confusion, excitement, fear, anticipation, happiness, and absolute uncertainty. Shy captured so many nuances of her feelings—it was such a beautiful statement.

Over the next few days as I stayed in the hospital, Sumant and I made a conscious effort to spend time alone with Tara and let her work through her emotions. Of course, by the second interaction with Leela, she was more curious and wanted to understand why she was "drinking from my tummy."

It was 2 weeks after I came home when Tara finally asked when Leela would leave. Despite our efforts to try to maintain her routine while also including her in caring for Leela, Tara was not so charmed by all the changes in our house and people's fascination with the little baby who had invaded her space. She had had enough.

When I was finally up to it, I decided to take Tara out to lunch, just the two of us, to have a mother-daughter heart-to-heart. Tara asked again about Leela's plan to leave. I told Tara that Leela was now a part of our family, and I knew Tara was going to be a great big sister. Tara still seemed unsure.

So I asked Tara if she would still sit in my lap and cuddle with me at night. If she would still let me tickle her tummy after her bath and sing songs and dance together in the evenings. I asked her if I could still call her my *jaan* (my life) and my special, darling baby. I asked her if I could give her a gazillion kisses every day and hug her so I could stay warm and happy.

Tara gave me a big, warm smile. She was still as special and as loved as before.

Question for Your Child:

How can you show your baby brother or sister that you love them?

33

Why are they laughing at me?

From a very young age, Tara had a prolonged and, what seemed to me, heightened sense of stranger anxiety. Thinking back, it seems almost comical how she would scream when certain people looked at her, with a smile, and said how sweet she was. At one point, we concluded that Indian men with moustaches were completely off-limits socially for us, because she would panic when she saw them! Only other parents could understand it when they saw Sumant and I wandering outside a restaurant or a party trying to calm her down from unknown fears.

I would question my parenting philosophy over and over again—should I calm her down, protect her, take her out of the situation and make her feel safe, or should I make her face her fears and realize that the Indian men with moustaches were not so evil after all?

As Tara was able to use her words more and more, she started to verbalize her fears and the reasons behind them more clearly. One day, we were in a bustling restaurant and she began to panic—she finally told me that she thought a group of women chatting and giggling at a table next to us were laughing at her. No matter how much I tried to convince her otherwise, she was determined that they were laughing at her. "Mommy, why are they laughing at me?"

I was telling my cousin, then 23 years old, about Tara's random fear, and she told me that she remembered very clearly having the same sense of panic when she was young that people were laughing at her. She said that panic had stayed with her to this day.

It was a reminder to me that our children's emotions and interactions are very real, whether we understand them or not. Tara's fear was genuine. As her mother, I needed to make her feel safe and loved and protected. So, if she really believed that the women at the table next to us were laughing at her, I needed to hold her through that moment of insecurity, not convince her about a different reality. And, later, when the fear had passed, we could talk more about how people interact and that people laugh when they are happy.

34

Why are you shouting at me?

When I had a second child, everyone told me that it would get exponentially harder. But to be honest, I didn't find it that difficult in the beginning. Leela, as an infant, slept and fed well, and Tara was an easy child always eager to help. I would quietly pat myself on the back, giving myself credit for having such calm, easy children.

It was when Leela turned 1 and Tara was approaching 4 that things began to change. On one hand, they began to play more with each other. Tara suddenly discovered that her baby sister would do what she said and follow her, and Tara loved to direct her! Sumant and I would watch them lovingly as they hugged and played hide-and-seek and laughed with each other. On the other hand, Tara noticed that her cute sister was getting much more attention now that she was beginning to talk, smile, joke, and move, and Tara became much more needy.

If Leela wanted to sit in my lap, so did Tara. If I kissed Leela, Tara would cry, "Why aren't you kissing me?" If someone admired Leela's baby outfit, Tara would push herself in front to make sure hers was admired. And Leela, like any other baby sibling, made sure that she got the attention she deserved. She was quite strong and unintimidated by her big sister's desire to overshadow her.

Aside from the competitiveness, I also found that our life was finding a new rhythm. Tara was going to school for a few hours a week, and I suddenly realized what the "soccer mom" lifestyle encompassed. School, activities, managing the house, food, groceries, paying bills—I realized that as my children grew older, the demands were only getting greater. I was constantly telling the kids to do one thing or not do another. I was always cleaning up only to find that things were a mess 2 minutes later. I was behind on my bills, we never had the right food, and the laundry was piling up. And my temper was getting shorter.

One day, I was tired and frustrated, and trying to focus on getting an article written that was overdue. In the background, Tara was whining about something that Leela had done and had pushed her down, so Leela was crying. I snapped at Tara not to hurt her sister, and told her that Mama was trying to work, why couldn't she just try to help me out?

"Why are you shouting at me?" she cried back at me.

I stopped for a moment. Was I shouting? I had to admit I had, and I had done it unconsciously. Tara continued, "You're not the ruler of me! You can't shout at me and tell me what to do!"

There was no explanation I could give Tara other than the fact that I had made a mistake. Mama was tired and frustrated and confused. When Tara asked, "Why are you tired and frustrated and confused?" I knew it was time for me to look at my life and make some changes. I had promised myself to always remember that my children were my most precious gift from God, and I needed to act that way.

35

Why are you and Papa fighting?

T ara asked, "Why are you and Papa fighting?"

Sumant and I were having a disagreement and were irritated with each other. But, not wanting to fight in front of the children, we were consciously not talking to each other about the matter at hand.

"We're not fighting, Baby," I told her. I picked up Leela, who was being a bit more clingy than usual.

I asked Sumant if I should put a waffle in for breakfast.

He said, "Sure."

Tara looked at both of us and asked again, "Mom, why are you and Papa fighting?"

I couldn't help myself as I smiled at Sumant. Of course she and Leela knew we were fighting! They did not need to hear the words. They could feel the tension in the air. They truly knew how to feel the universe and trust their intuition.

Tara's question made me realize once again that our children are listening not only to our words, but are also watching and feeling and interpreting our actions, our thoughts, our intentions. There will always be moments when they feel our anger, sadness, frustration, or confusion. I decided that it was best to be truthful.

I admitted that Mama and Papa were fighting. But I told her we were talking about our disagreement and would work it out. She understood. I reassured her that Papa and I still loved each other, and that we just needed some time to find the right words. As I uttered these explanations, Sumant touched my shoulder and the tension eased. We both smiled at our angelic daughter, and all three of us knew that everything would be okay.

Question for Your Child: _____

How can we tell someone we love that we are angry with them?

_____

36

Why doesn't anyone want to play with me?

The questions that make my heart break are the ones that indicate a hint of insecurity or a desire that I cannot fulfill.

Why doesn't she want to sit next to me? Why are the other kids making fun of me? Why doesn't anyone want to play with me?

Most times, I cannot deny the reality of the situation. Kids in school always seem to have their preferences, and they are ever changing. One day, Tara wants to sit with one friend, and another day she doesn't want to talk to her. Her friend may be hurt and confused by the change. Often, the result is tears—hurt by one child, and a renewed commitment by the other one to stick to their decision. As a mom, I try to justify and apologize to her hurt friend as I am trying to console my crying daughter.

I watch with amazement as teachers help the children in the classroom negotiate with each other. They ask the children to be nice to their friends, to recognize their feelings, encouraging them to be nice. They have a language that helps the children to empathize with other kids' desires. Observing and listening to school teachers, I have learned the benefits of reassuring words, provoking questions, and affirmations for good behavior.

But the reality is that children are often mean to each other. They realize they can push buttons in each other, and they test them on purpose. How do I teach my daughters to be immune to others' hurtful comments? How do I teach them to know their inherent goodness and beauty without needing the approval of others?

When Tara complains that no one wants to play with her, I ask her, "Is it that no one wants to play with you or that you want to play something different?" Often, she wants to play something different (she wants to play with her dolls, instead of kicking the ball), so the question helps her realize that she is just not getting what she wants. "Sweetie, they are playing with the ball. Perhaps you can play ball right now, and later someone will play with the dolls with you."

In the situations where her friend really doesn't want to sit next to her, I try to convince her that her friend is just feeling like doing something else right now. It is not about Tara, but about what her friend is feeling at the moment. She needs to sit somewhere else today. I tell Tara that Mama would really be happy if she sat next to me instead.

And, in the difficult scenarios where someone has truly been mean to her, I first hold her and make her feel loved. We then talk about how when people are mean, they are probably hurting themselves. So maybe we need to see that they are hurt and realize it has nothing to do with us. We can be nice to them to make them feel better or we can just ignore them.

We can't always protect our children from being hurt. But perhaps if we take the time to work through the particular situation, we can influence the way they will react in similar situations for the rest of their lives.

37

Can he be my brother?

In India, there is a festival called Rakhi that celebrates the relationships between brothers and sisters. A sister ties a red string on her brother's wrist, and the brother vows to protect her for life. Traditionally, the festival includes extended families, and girls will send rakhi threads to both their brothers and their boy cousins. In return, the brother or boy cousin sends the girl a gift.

One day as Rakhi was approaching, I was opening up the mail and setting aside the rakhis that had been sent by my husband's cousins—he has nine girl cousins!

To my surprise, a rakhi had also come from one of our dear friends. In the letter, she wrote to Sumant about how he had become a big brother to her over the years, being there for her during a particularly challenging time in her life.

It was a lovely testament to friendship and family—that in life, we are born with certain members in our family whom we are connected to no matter what, but that we also have the choice to open ourselves to others and establish new, meaningful bonds. By sending Sumant a rakhi, our friend had performed a ritual that expressed her commitment and love for him in a way that was deeper than words.

38

How do I remember people whom I miss?

Nana was my grandparent who was the most active in playing games and taking us to visit museums, parks, zoos, and sites. For all the grandchildren, Nana was our closest companion and playmate. To this day, Nana, who is now 85 years old, remains the favorite playmate for his great-grandchildren.

I used to play a game with my grandfather that always made me giggle. It began when I was about 7 years old and had traveled alone to London with Nana and Nani (my grandmother). My grandparents diligently took me around the city to see all the famous sites.

After taking me to Cleopatra's Needle, Nana sang, "Now don't say you haven't seen Cleopatra's Needle!"

I smiled and mischievously asked, "Nana, when are we going to see Cleopatra's Needle?"

And Nana put his hand to his head and laughed, "Ohhh noo!"

So began a game that continued for every site or place we visited for the next few years. Without fail, whenever we saw a new place, Nana would sing his line,

"Now don't say you haven't seen…" And I would respond with my question and a giggle.

When Tara was almost 5, we were on holiday in Mexico and had gone to see the bay of Puerto Vallarta. When we were leaving, I told her about the game I used to play with my grandfather, Nana. I finished by saying to her, "Tara, now don't say that you haven't seen Puerto Vallarta!" Tara caught on immediately and asked, "But Mama, when are we going to see Puerto Vallarta?"

As I sang, "Ohh noo!" I had a flood of memories of the many games and giggles with my grandfather. I felt connected to him. I hugged my daughter as I thought about how we could play this game for years to come and in doing so remain connected to the generations that came before us!

39

Do I remind you of someone?

"**D**id you know that when I hear you tell your long stories with so many twists and turns, I think about my grandfather, Daddy?" I said to Tara.

"Tell me more." Tara leaned forward, eyes open, anticipating a good story. She loved to hear about her family.

"When I see Leela's curly hair, I think about my beautiful Maa, who had such fine, curly hair." More and more, Leela reminded me of my grandmother. She had the same passion as her as well.

I stroked Tara's long, beautiful hair. "And Dadiji, your grandfather's mother, she loves to dress up like you. She is elegant and sophisticated. When Leela dances, I remember Dadiji dancing at my wedding, joyful, carefree, laughing." It was one of my fondest memories.

My daughter, Tara, was a devoted friend; she loved to write letters to her friends, look at photographs, and remember fun moments. "When you talk about your friends and I hear how much you love them, I smile remembering the stories that your papa's grandfather, Bhare Papa, used to tell us about his friends and how he loved them." Sumant's grandfather was a committed friend. After Sumant and I got married, he made a concentrated effort to become friends with my grandfather.

I gave Tara a piece of chocolate. "Did you know your love of chocolate and all things sweet is from Bhari Nani, my grandmother? Did you know that she loves to bake cookies and cakes and brownies just like you?" We had continued the tradition started by my grandmother of baking cakes for all our family members.

"When you do your arts and crafts projects, it reminds me of your father's grandmother, Naniji. Remember those blankets she made for you? They were made with love and attention—I see the same emotion in you when you make your cards for those you love."

"And, Sweetie, your sharp memory, it is just like your papa's grandfather, Dadaji. He could remember everything, and he loved his books, just like you."

I looked at Tara and Leela, and heard and felt and saw the voices, the memories, the emotions, and the movements of all those who had been part of their creation.

40

Why do you say everything is everything?

I like to illustrate to Tara and Leela ways in which we are connected to everything else. When we feel a connection to other people and places and things, we develop a sense of respect for them.

We were sitting on a wooden bench at the park. I pondered out loud, "I wonder where this bench came from?"

"It's made from wood, Mama. Wood from a tree," Tara graciously explained.

"So I wonder if that tree lived in Africa or India or China or Switzerland or Brazil or here in the United States!" One could marvel at the places and connections that could be made.

"Maybe from Egypt, Mama! Because there is a lot of sun there to shine on the trees." Tara's eyes were wide with excitement. I had an image of oak trees in the sprawling desert.

"That's true. The tree would need the sun and water to grow so that its wood would be strong enough." We made the connection with the environment.

"And I wonder if the wood was taken to carpenters who lived somewhere else, perhaps in Sweden. And if those carpenters asked their friends from Japan for designs for a good bench." Tara nodded her head animatedly and looked at the design of the bench.

"And then someone who manages this park had to find the perfect bench for mamas and kids to sit on…" I opened up the question for her as to how the bench got to the park.

"Maybe she saw it in a catalog, like all those catalogs we get at home." Probably true, I nodded.

"And then she had to order it, and a delivery person had to bring it to this park."

"Like a mailman?" Tara asked.

"Yes, a special sort of mailman," I said.

Tara and I took another look at the bench, and Tara stroked it as she admired its work. Indeed, it had taken the earth, the elements, different places, and different people to bring the bench into our little park.

How Do People Interact with Each Other?

Luca: "What are the magic words?"

Luca's aunt: "Thank you!"

Luca: "No. The magic words are 'cake mix.'"

LUCA (AGE 3)

41

Mommy, what's a bomb?

It was a typical morning.

Leela, 9 months old, tossed and turned for a while before finally demanding that I get out of bed and pick her up. Sumant stretched in bed, and Tara called, "Mom, I woke up!" We all cuddled in bed for a while and then got up to make breakfast.

I put the television on, and there were images from the London bombings flashing one after another. Sumant and I were dead silent.

Tara asked me a question. I didn't pay attention, so absorbed was I in trying to decipher what was going on. Leela was screeching with delight, having found a carrot from the night before under the sofa.

A typical morning, but not really.

Tara pulled at me again, "Mommy, what's a bomb?" Finally, my 3-year-old had caught my attention.

I turned the television off and held my daughters. I looked at Sumant, not knowing how to answer.

I looked at the innocence in both my daughters' eyes. The look of pure love, pure trust, and pure compassion.

How do you explain that bad things happen? That there are people who purposefully kill and hurt others?

I held both girls in my lap, held them to feel their love, to feel stronger, to know that they would process the information from a place of compassion. I held on to them, and knew that it was their purity of spirit that held hope for the future.

"Sometimes, Baby, people hurt others because they are hurting themselves..." I stumbled in my explanation, but continued. "And sometimes they may do things that not only hurt other people's feelings, but also their homes or towns." I did not want to be graphic or create a fear in Tara about a world that she trusted.

"Isn't that naughty, Mama?"

"Yes, Baby, it is naughty."

"Are people going to hurt us?" Tara proceeded to ask.

"No," I assured her. We could not live in fear. "But it is important for us to remember that we need to respect others, to listen and to understand their feelings. If we respect other people, perhaps they won't hurt so much."

I held on tight to my precious little girls, thinking about how their future was inextricably tied to the actions, words, and understanding of my generation.

42

Why does he have two fathers?

Tara has two friends, who are twins, who live with their gay fathers. One of their fathers is their biological father, and the other father is their adopted father. The surrogate mother who carried them is an integral part of their family, playing the role of an aunt. They are growing up in a very loving, secure, and happy environment. They are surrounded by people who listen to them, care for them, teach them good values, hold them, and keep them safe.

Tara has another friend whose parents are going through a divorce. The little girl lives between her mother's and father's homes, both parents dedicated to their daughter's well-being.

She has another friend, a girl from China, who was adopted by a single professional mom. Her mother is now planning on adopting another baby, perhaps from India or Ethiopia.

While society debates gay marriages, adoption requirements, and the consequences of divorce, I have watched Tara accept different families with ease. Watching Tara accept her friends, no matter where they come from, has been one of the most important lessons in tolerance for me.

She asks questions, she processes my explanations, and most important, she observes her friends. When a situation seems different to her—like when her friend looks different from her mother or has two fathers—she asks questions without judgment or prejudice. She often seeks clarity, insight, or more information. And her acceptance of those situations is based on my answers, my body language, and the tone of my voice.

Question for Your Child

What is a family?

43

What does adoption mean?

Tara's friend, Mango, asked her mother what adoption means. Mango had heard that one of her friends in preschool was adopted, but didn't understand what that actually meant.

Her mother told her that sometimes a mama and papa cannot take care of their child—maybe the parents are too young, they don't have enough money, they need to ask someone else to help them. So they ask a nice family to take care of their baby, and the baby becomes part of a new family. The baby gets a mama and papa who can take care of them and love them just like Mango's mother loves Mango.

Mango listened intently, and her mother hoped she had answered the question sensitively and truthfully.

The next day, Mango and her mother were at the toy store and Mango wanted to buy several toys. Mango's mother told her that she could buy one toy, but not too many. Mango asked why she couldn't buy too many toys. Her mother told her that they didn't want to waste money, which she and Mango's father worked hard to make.

Mango thought really hard, and then she quietly asked her mother, "Mommy, if we run out of money, will you have to give me up for adoption?"

Mango's mother held her baby close. "No, Baby, no. No matter what happens, I won't give you away."

"But then why do some mamas give their babies away?" Mango asked again. She was still trying to resolve her uncertainty from the day before.

"Sometimes, Baby, people don't have a choice. Or they find a family that will love the baby as much as they do, and give her things they cannot."

She continued, "But your daddy and I are lucky and will always be able to take care of you."

Mango was still struggling to resolve her uncertainty, and her mama realized that some questions just take longer for little ones to understand.

44

Why is that man looking through our trash?

We were driving out of our garage one afternoon and a homeless man was rummaging through our trash, looking for food and recyclable bottles. Tara immediately sat upright, as she looked out her window, and the man consciously ignored us. He was making a mess, tearing the bags open. I had noticed flies congregating around my trash and had once commented that I found it irritating.

"Why is that man in our house? Why is he taking things from our trash? Mama, look at the mess he is making."

Three immediate thoughts came to me as I thought about how to respond to her.

The first was about boundaries. What separated us from that man that Tara considered him to be "in our house."

The second thought took me back to when Tara was just 6 months old and reminded me about kindness when she smiled at a homeless man on the street, not judging him.

The third was the reminder that my kids were always listening to me. At 6 months, she smiled at the homeless man. At 4 years old, she was beginning to process and question and interpret situations. She was following my example. I thought about my comments about the mess making me mad.

As I closed the garage, I opened the window. I called out, "Excuse me. Excuse me, sir…" The man continued to ignore me. "Please, sir," I persisted. He glanced at me, sideways, hesitatingly.

"I have no problem with you going through our trash," I started. Tara watched intently. The man finally looked at me. "It's just that the mess is attracting a lot of flies…" I listened to myself and thought it was a lame way to engage him in conversation.

I began again. "I have no problem with you going through our trash. But, since the flies bug me, I will start separating the food and recyclables. Maybe that will make life easier for both of us."

"Works for me," he replied.

I closed the window and continued down the alley. I could see Tara processing all that had happened. And before I could say anything, she said, "Mama, that was good. Now you are both working together."

Question for Your Child

How do we get our food on our table?

45

Why was the black man shooting a gun?

We were in Miami for a wedding and were walking to the ocean when there was a major commotion in an open building complex. We heard a man say, "Put your hands up. This is the police." Sirens screamed as cars raced around the corner, and we heard gun shots just about 50 yards from us.

Mommy emergency mode—that base survival instinct—took over. I swept up Tara, who was holding my hand, into my arms and shouted to my mom, brother, sister-in-law, and husband to run. My mom was pushing Leela in a stroller, and in an instant, Sumant was running, pushing the stroller ahead of him.

We turned the corner and finally stopped to catch our breath when we were out of range from the mayhem. Everyone was absolutely fine, and we actually chuckled about having a true Miami experience!

Tara, who had not panicked at all, but rather seemed to have enjoyed the run with me, was listening intently to us. She was about 3½ years old. Before I could begin an explanation of what had just happened, she asked an unnerving question.

"Mama, why was the black man shooting a gun?"

My mother, Gotham, Candice, Sumant, and I looked at each other. None of us had even noticed what was happening, let alone seen who was doing what. We just wanted to get out of there.

What had Tara seen? What had just seemed like a good story to tell about Miami now concerned me as I panicked about its impression on my daughter. Also, I was taken aback that she had identified the man as black. When did she start to notice and distinguish the color of people's skin?

"Did you see a man shooting a gun?" I carefully asked.

"The black man outside was pointing his gun at the door. Why was the black man shooting a gun? Was he a naughty man, Mama?" Tara was at the age where she always wanted to know if characters in movies were naughty or nice.

So many thoughts whirled in my head as Tara looked at me for some guidance. Aside from thinking about how to explain to her what had just happened, I realized that she was creating an association: black man—gun—naughty.

I had to tackle the question from my gut. "Tara, actually the black man was a nice man. He was a policeman and he was trying to protect us."

"Why was he shooting the gun?"

"Because sometimes policemen, to do their jobs, use guns."

"But I thought guns were bad." I realized Sumant and I had reinforced this concept when talking about guns when, by chance, Tara had been exposed to them through the media. Thus, guns equaled naughty in Tara's innocent mind.

"Sometimes, even good people use guns when they have no choice." I felt like

I was not making any sense.

Tara and I continued the dialogue, talking through what had happened, with me and Sumant and my mother attempting to carefully and consciously answer her poignant questions.

It literally took months for Tara to process the whole experience—months of questioning, months of reiterating that the black man was good, months of talking through the same experience and the same line of questioning. Even a year later, when someone mentioned Miami, Tara said, "Mama, remember that black man who was shooting the gun?" She would pause for a moment, and then say, "He was good and protecting us, but had to use the gun."

I still wonder if I handled this situation with Tara appropriately. The whole experience emphasized how every interaction a child has influences his or her worldview. Reiterating to Tara that the black man was a good policeman hopefully would create a fundamental positive association and judgment about society for her.

My desire was to teach Tara and Leela to be open, compassionate, and tolerant. To do so required me to be patient when answering their questions, face the hard ones, and help them come to terms with things at their own pace.

46

Why can't I get the shoes I want?

I had taken the girls to buy shoes. Both loved shoes—Tara always wanted pink ones, and Leela was just thrilled to be in a room full of endless shoes.

Tara chose two pairs of shoes to try on while Leela ran around the store singing, "Shoes! Shoes!" Before I could even look at the price, the salesman had gone into the back room to find Tara's size.

As the salesman put the first pair of shoes on her, I saw that my fashion-conscious daughter had chosen a very cool, very expensive pair of designer shoes. The salesman was telling her how beautiful they were, that she looked like a real princess in them. Tara glowed with pride. I hesitatingly watched.

"Tara, try the other pair of shoes on," I encouraged her. As he put the shoes on her, the salesman was not as enthusiastic. And, in turn, neither was Tara—even though they were also pink and shiny.

Tara looked at me and clearly stated that she wanted the designer pair. When I looked at the price, I winced. They were more expensive than shoes I had ever bought for myself.

"Baby, I don't think we can buy these shoes. Let's get the other pair."

Tara's eyes filled up with tears, and her voice was quivering as she hugged the designer shoes. "But I want these shoes." I could see the salesman smiling next to me. I could also sense a tantrum coming.

As a mother, I often struggled with my desire to give my children everything. More important, however, I wanted to teach them values that were important to me.

"Tara, we are not going to buy those shoes. If you don't want the other shoes, we can wait until we find a pair of shoes that you do want," I said firmly.

"But I want these shoes!" she screamed back. The tears were rolling down her cheeks now, and Leela had stopped her shoe song.

"Tara, these shoes are too expensive. We are not going to buy them."

"I don't care. What does expensive mean? I want them now!" she screamed. At this point, the salesman realized I wasn't a gullible customer and he focused on some other clients.

I sat down and took Tara in my lap. "Expensive means that they cost too much money. Mama and Papa work really hard to make money so that we can live in a nice house, eat good food, and buy you and your sister special things."

"But Mama, I really want these shoes. They are very special."

I continued. "I know they are special, Tara. But we have to choose what we are going to spend money on. If we buy these shoes, then we may not be able to buy dinner or a sweater when it is cold or get you a new doll. Or we may not be able to buy your sister shoes. That wouldn't be nice, would it? We have to decide what is most important to us."

"Mommy, the shoes are the most important things to me. I don't want anything else. I don't want dinner. I only want the shoes." Tara was not backing down.

"I know you want those shoes, darling. But sometimes even if we want something really badly, like these shoes, we can't get them right away. Sometimes, we have to wait to get them or we decide that they really aren't that important. And even if you decide you don't want your dinner, your sister needs to eat her dinner. That is important, no?"

Tara was still unhappy, but she did put down the shoes. I decided to leave before we made more of a scene.

She sat silently in the car. "Are you okay, Baby?" I asked.

She was still sulking, but also thinking.

Finally, she said, "Maybe, after dinner, we can go to the other store and see if there are some nice shoes for both me and Leela. Shoes that are not too *extansive*."

Good idea, I smiled.

Question for Your Child

When you want two things, how do you choose which one you want?

47

How come she can't sit with us?

During a visit to India, Tara had a playdate with a friend. Her friend, also 4 years old, came to the house with her *aya* (nanny). Her *aya*, probably 15 years old, was from a poor family and stayed with Tara's friend day and night. She was her constant companion, supporting the mother and managing the little girl's every need. By living with Tara's friend, she was able to support herself and her family, and likely avoid scary situations that a poor young girl could face.

When we sat down for dinner, the *aya* stood by the door, watching us eat. If the little girl dropped some food on the ground, she would quickly scamper in, pick up the food, and tell the girl to eat nicely. Then, with a shy smile on her face, she would return to the doorway.

"Mama, why isn't she eating with us?" Tara asked, after the *aya* had made her second trip to clean up some food from the floor.

How do I answer this? It took a moment to gather my thoughts.

In a culture where hierarchies often seem to form the fabric of the economy, culture, and society, such a scenario is not out of the ordinary. It is a system that seems to work, supporting the needs and survival of different classes of society.

Before I could respond, Tara's friend laughed. "She can't sit with us!" Tara looked more confused, and looked at me for an answer.

Her friend continued, "She has to eat in the kitchen when we are done."

Tara asked again, "Mama, why does she have to eat separately?"

I had no idea what to say. It was a much larger question. A question about what I believed in, about how I wanted to teach my children to interact with the world.

Should I be teaching them that certain things are as they are and we must accept them? That it is important for us to respect different traditions?

Or should I be encouraging her to ask questions and try to change things? After all, if no one asked questions, wouldn't people still have to sit at the back of the bus or be excluded from restaurants in their own land?

I looked at the faces of the two innocent girls looking at me. "Sweetie, I think her *aya* wants to help her eat first. Then, when she eats her dinner, she can enjoy her food." I knew I was telling a half-truth, but it felt like the right approach at that moment.

"No, Auntie," Tara's precocious friend responded. "She *has* to help me first, and then when I am done, she can eat in the kitchen." I had not been prepared for the push back.

"Actually, she has made the choice to take care of you," I firmly replied. "And it is important that we always respect her choices, just like we respect each other's choices."

Tara's friend shrugged her shoulders and continued to eat her food. I could see

Tara trying to process the interaction and what I had said.

And I admittedly was shaken—shaken by the reminder that the world was a complicated place with different points of view and approaches to life. I felt the awesome responsibility of what it meant to be a mother—a mother who influenced the worldview of my children. The challenge for me was to share my perspective with my children, while not being judgmental about how other people interacted with their world. Tara's friend had a worldview shaped by her family and society, and at some level, I felt I had to respect that. At the same time, I had to show my children that I stood by my beliefs so that they too would be able to stand by their own ideals. I hoped that by facing the world together and not being apprehensive about talking about the difficult questions, we would grow, evolve, and learn together.

48

Why is that baby lying naked
on the side of the road?

We were waiting at a traffic light in our air-conditioned car on a hot New Delhi afternoon when a woman tapped on our window. She was wearing a ragged sari, her hair was in a loose braid, and her expression was melancholy. As she begged for money, she pushed her malnourished baby, who was wrapped in a dirty rag, to the window, and asked for food for her child.

The woman mesmerized Tara, 4 years old. "Mama, what does she want? Why is her baby not wearing any clothes? Why is that baby lying on the road?" I looked at the side of the road, and indeed there were two more children—a little girl, Tara's age, sitting with an infant in her little lap.

A barrage of questions. Disturbing images. A reality that had no comforting answers.

The woman, seeing Tara's reaction and my momentary helplessness, tapped harder. Her baby cried.

"She is asking us for money to help her children." It was the truth. As a mother, I empathized with this woman's desperation to beg for money for her children.

However, I hesitated to give her some money, knowing that many times these beggars were controlled by the Mafia and did not keep most of the money they got at street corners.

"Why does she need money, Mama? Why aren't her children wearing clothes? Why can't you help her?" Tara only had questions, and she was visibly confused.

I felt completely helpless and at a loss for words. Why couldn't I help this mother and her children? What separated me, sitting in my fancy air-conditioned car, from her? Why were we so lucky, and why was her family lacking so much?

"Baby, this woman is asking for help in the only way she knows how. Her family doesn't have all the things that we have…We are lucky that we always have food and toys and nice clothes." I really didn't know what to say.

"Do you think we should give her some money?" I asked.

"Yes, Mama. Maybe that will help her a little bit. Maybe she can buy her daughter a pretty doll like mine," Tara replied deep in thought.

So I rolled down the window and handed the woman some money. She quickly moved on to the next car, hoping to get some more cash before the traffic light turned green.

Question for Your Child

How can we help those who are not as fortunate as we are?

49

Why can't I have blond hair and blue eyes?

One afternoon, Tara's friend came home from school upset. She cried, "Mommy, why can't I have blond hair and blue eyes?" Tara's friend was South Asian—a pretty little girl with thick black hair, beautiful dark eyes, and lovely brown skin.

Her mother held her, wondering what had happened to create this outburst. So her mother asserted how beautiful she was, and that she looked just as she was meant to be.

But the question continued for the next few days. After some prying, her friend's mother deducted that during dress-up at school, another girl had told her daughter that she couldn't be a princess, because she did not have blond hair and blue eyes. After all, the girls considered Cinderella and Sleeping Beauty the most beautiful princesses, and they had fair skin, blue eyes, and blond hair.

I realized that in our household, as well, Tara had identified with these classic, blond-haired, blue-eyed princesses. Tara did not care much for Disney's latest attempts with multicultural princesses—Mulan and Pocahontas—because neither of them wore the long flowing dresses, like the other ones. For Tara, it was about the beautiful clothes that these girls wore—for now, she could be a princess by wearing those clothes. For Tara's friend, it had become about the color of their skin, hair, and eyes—but she could not change those aspects of herself.

This experience stressed to me how much media and pop culture define our sense of self, starting at a very early age. While, as South Asian parents, we made bold attempts to give our children a sense of pride in their Indian heritage—through movies and clothes, festivals, travel and gatherings with other children—we could not protect them from a dominant society that hinted they were not as good or pretty or special. The same was true of children who were black or East Asian. And the messages continued through the depiction of women with perfect faces and bodies in magazines and movies.

The girl at school was probably innocently commenting on her reality of princesses, not realizing how it hurt and excluded her friend who looked different. The interaction was a reminder for me about the importance of stressing, over and over again, day after day, to my daughters that we all are special and beautiful in our own way. I also decided to take responsibility to educate the other parents and children in our lives about such diversity by organizing cultural activities at school and inviting Tara and Leela's friends and families home for dinner. Perhaps it was one way that I could stress to my daughters and their friends that beauty comes in many guises.

Question for Your Child

If we could visit one new place in the world, where would you want to go?

50

What do I do when I am frustrated?

I was having a particularly rough day, facing a number of challenges with my various professional projects. The pressure was building up, and finally I just snapped by fighting for no reason with my brother, father, and husband. I was demanding and rude and blaming them for things they had not done. (I work with my brother and father on projects, and well, my husband is my husband.)

After I had some time to think about my reaction, I recalled telling Tara the day before to use her words when she was frustrated. And I had to admit that I was forgetting to use my own words and instead, letting all the frustration build up inside of me.

When we were young and got upset about something, my father would wait until we got out of our agitated state before addressing the issue at hand. As we grew older, he articulated a process for nonviolent communication that was very useful to me. It incorporated a process of evaluating a feeling, identifying a need, determining how to fulfill that need, and then communicating that need and vulnerability to the relevant person.

When I reflected on this process, I realized that, in essence, I was asking my children on a daily basis to use their words and tell me what they wanted. And my children generally did a pretty good job of articulating their feelings and needs. In fact, they probably did a better job than most adults, including myself. Indeed, couldn't one say that many conflicts stemmed from not using our words and expressing our needs early on?

If my goal as a mother and as an individual was to nurture a peaceful society for my family, it was important for me to keep using my words, rather than let the pressure build to the tipping point. The first step was to apologize to those I loved for taking out my frustration on them. And then I made a commitment to articulate my needs both to myself and those around me so that we could interact in a more loving, harmonious, and effective manner.

Question for Your Child

What can you do when you feel frustrated?

What Kind of Choices Do I Have?

"Mom, when are they going
to stop making days?"

Téa (age 4)

51

Do I have to color inside the lines?

Tara and Leela love to color and paint.

One afternoon, we were playing with paper, coloring books, and a box of crayons. We taped a blank piece of paper on the table for Leela, who pushed the crayon hard against the paper and went back and forth. Leela was just beginning to label colors and shrieked with delight as she saw the "buu" (blue) color appear.

Tara, meanwhile, sat seriously in her little red chair at the table and was flipping through a coloring book. She finally chose a picture—a princess, of course—and set it carefully on the table. She looked at the picture intently, and I thought she was contemplating which color to use for the dress.

"Mama," she began, "why do I have to color inside the lines?" She continued looking at the picture before her.

Interesting question, I thought to myself. We are taught at a very young age that we are supposed to color inside the lines. We are taught to color the sky shades of blue, the grass green, and the sun yellow. We practice and practice and practice coloring inside the lines and are rewarded with compliments when we do it perfectly. But coloring inside the lines with the right colors trains us to think like everyone else. Is coloring inside the lines training our children to think inside the box?

I watched Leela coloring. She was completely free, full of joy as she splashed colors on her white paper. Absolute creativity and playfulness and free-flowing expression.

"You know what, Tara, why do we have to color inside the lines? Perhaps we can let the color flow outside the lines this time. What do you think?"

Tara smiled. Sounded good. "Mama. Maybe sometimes we will color in the lines, and sometimes we will not. We can decide for every picture how we want to do it. Or even do it half and half."

Whatever you want, my darling, I told her.

And Leela continued her coloring. This time, fascinated by the color "wed" (red).

Question for Your Child

How many colors can you see in the sky?

52

What if I fall down?

My natural tendency as a mother is to want to help my daughters in any situation. I find it difficult to actually watch them struggle—from the simple task of getting a ball from under the table to screwing a cap on a bottle. In my heart, I know they need to figure things out. In my mind, I tell myself to let them learn. My actions, however, often betray my desires. Frequently, I have to remind myself to stand back and let them fall every once in a while so that they can learn and gain strength from getting up again.

Tara was learning how to ride a bike. We had bought her a new, pink bike that fit all the specifications for a princess. A matching pink helmet and pink jogging pants added to the excitement.

When we got on the road, though, Tara was very apprehensive.

Don't let go!

Mama, keep holding the handle!

Don't let me fall!

Her focus was making sure that I was protecting her, rather than trying to push the pedal.

"Sweetie, don't worry. I won't let go. You focus on riding the bike."

As she became more comfortable, I tried to let go of the handle. Immediately she cried, "Don't let go, Mama! I will fall."

"I won't let you fall," I reassured her. Tara gained confidence and rode half a block. She was thrilled.

But, then she fell. A melodramatic scene occurred—she wasn't really hurt, but she was upset that I had let go. I had told her I wouldn't let her fall, and she had fallen. And I had no excuse. The reality was I could never promise her that she would not fall again.

With the tears wiped away, I tried to get Tara excited again about getting on the bike. "See, Sweetie. You did such a great job! Let's try again." She was a bit resistant.

"But, what if I fall again?" she asked.

"You know what, let's focus on getting up and trying again. And I will help you and not let go until you are ready. Okay?"

She tentatively agreed. "But don't let go. Promise me you won't let go, because I don't want to fall again."

I stood beside her on the bike. I couldn't make that promise. "Sweetie, I will help you until you are ready. Let's remember what happened when you fell, and try not to do it again."

Tara thought. "I think I fell because I forgot not to ride on the grass."

"See, we can learn something each time we fall!" We were ready to ride again.

Still a bit apprehensive, Tara agreed to try again. And this time, when she reached the end of the block, her face beamed with pride. She had actually done it!

53

How do we use money?

When Leela turned 1, it became more obvious how she was soaking in information. She repeated words, mimicked expressions and gestures, and copied everything that we did (especially everything her big sister did!). And I realized as I watched my little toddler discover her world that everything that I did really set the stage for how she would perceive the objects and people around her.

One day, Leela discovered coins. When I pointed to the quarter and said, "Money," she carefully repeated the word once. I clapped my hands and cheered, "Yeah!" A big grin on her face, she now repeated, "Munee, munee, munee! Yeah!"

Continuing our game, I put the coins in my hand and shook them. Leela shook her shoulders, dancing to the rhythm of the coins. "Munee, munee! Dancee!" she squealed with delight.

Now, I changed the game a bit. I took the coins and put one in between each of her toes. She giggled and wiggled her toes. "Toesees! Munnee toesees!" Each time one fell out of her tiny baby toes, she pointed to it and demanded, "Munee toesees!"

For the next few months, every time Leela found coins, she went through the same routine. Jingling them, dancing, and then putting the coins in her toes. If she was wearing shoes and socks, both had to come off so that the coins could be put in between her toes.

Leela was also not shy about putting the coins in other people's toes. Tara, Sumant, and I played and laughed along with her game, but other toddlers would sometimes get annoyed that Leela was trying to pull off their socks to pretty up their toes. In her little mind, coins were like any other piece of jewelry—pretty, shiny objects that were great decorations!

54

Can I have a waffle with syrup
and lots of cream cheese?

Tara generally wants one of two things for breakfast: waffles (usually without syrup), or a bagel with lots of cream cheese.

We have the same routine every morning. "Tara, what would you like for breakfast today?"

"Umm," she feigns to think. "A dry waffle."

"No syrup?" I ask.

"Nope."

And, every once in a while, she will respond with "A bagel with lots and lots of cream cheese."

One morning, however, she surprised me.

"Tara, what would you like for breakfast today?"

"Umm," she thought. "Today I would like a waffle with syrup and lots of cream cheese."

"You can't have a waffle with syrup and cream cheese," I laughed.

"Why?" She looked at me—big wide eyes, total innocence, and genuine questioning.

Why? I was about to say, "Just because." And then I realized what I was doing. Why couldn't she have waffles with syrup and lots of cream cheese? Just because I thought it would taste gross didn't mean that she wouldn't like it. She had the right to form her own opinions.

"Actually, that sounds like a really interesting combination! Will you help me make it?"

She jumped up, excited. We toasted the waffle. She spread a lot of cream cheese on it. She poured a lot of syrup. "Mmm. Looks good!" And then she took a bite. No reaction. She took another bite. "Maybe Leela wants some."

The next morning, I asked, "Tara, what would you like for breakfast today?"

"Umm," she replied. "A dry waffle, please."

Question for Your Child

Can we eat our lunch for breakfast?

55

Can you make my nightmares go away?

Tara has a vivid imagination. She is an observer who takes in minute details and then processes them to tell colorful stories. I found that Tara's imagination carried on into the nighttime to become adventurous dreams.

One morning, Tara woke up crying and shaking. I held her tight, asking her what had happened.

"Mama, I had a nightmare. There was a scary dinosaur who had come into our house."

She was genuinely scared, and I held her tight, telling her it was only a dream. Being a child who loves to dwell on her feelings (and enjoying the cuddling), Tara was not ready to let go of the nightmare. I decided to try a new tactic.

"Tell me, Tara, what did the dinosaur look like?"

She looked at me, pausing before answering. I could tell she was trying to figure out what I was doing. She decided to play along.

"He was really big, Mama." She spread out her hands wide.

"Really! What color was he?" I responded.

"He was red and had pink polka dots! Can you believe it?"

"I have never heard of a red dinosaur with pink polka dots!" I laughed. "Did he have eyes?"

"Oh, yes. He had 364 eyes. All over his body!"

"My goodness! He must have been a funny-looking dinosaur!"

We continued our dialogue for 5 more minutes, describing the dinosaur in minute detail—the 587 teeth, the 16 ears, the 5 feet, and the sound of his roar.

We had faced the dinosaur together and realized that he was actually quite a funny character—quite clumsy, in fact, as he didn't know how to balance on his 16 legs, most of which were missing feet.

56

Mommy, why don't you listen to me?

A friend of mine sent me a poignant message about how our interactions with our children plant the seeds for a lifetime of emotion, learning, and connection. Coincidentally also named Tara, my friend sent me one of her free-flowing journal entries in which she processed her daughter's words to her about their relationship. She writes:

> I like it when I feel you hear me, Mommy—when you listen to what I am saying, when you hear what I want, what I am feeling, and what I need. Mommy, I need to feel listened to. When you look like you are not listening to me, I don't feel like you love me. If you loved me, you would stop and listen and respond to what I am saying, so that I feel like you can understand who I am and what my needs are, as well as Daddy's and Sister's and Brother's and everyone's. Mommy, I do not want to grow up feeling like you didn't stop to hear me, like I didn't count, because then, Mommy, I will not know how to take care of my own needs. I may not ever see what my needs really are.

Tara learned that she did not listen to her daughter, Elizabeth, when Elizabeth was little in the way she felt heard. When Elizabeth was 28, Mommy and Elizabeth sat down, and Mom finally listened. Mom heard, and did not defend herself, and listened to every word Elizabeth said. And Mom said, "I am so sorry I did not listen to you. Do you feel I listened to you now? Do you feel heard?" Elizabeth felt listened to and they forgave each other, and felt their relationship healed, and cried for the listening they had missed for so many years.

When I read Tara's entry and the lessons that she learned through listening attentively to her daughter, I felt emotion, but also relief. It made me forgive myself for not being the perfect mother. It reminded me that we are all just people doing our best, and that we have our vulnerabilities even though we love with all our hearts.

But it also emphasized to me that we make choices every day in our lives—choices to connect or not to connect, choices to forgive, and choices to love. We can reach out to make those connections in our lives at any and every moment.

Question for Your Child

What makes a person a good listener?

57

Does Nana really know the tooth fairy?

Tara asked me one day if Nana (my father) really knew the tooth fairy. In her voice, I could hear awe, wonder, magic, and hope.

"He does," I replied. "How did you find out that he knew her?"

"Nani told me." Nani is my mother. "She said Nana has known the tooth fairy for a really, really long time." There was not a tremor of doubt about the existence of the tooth fairy as she stated these words. In fact, she uttered them almost in a whisper, emphasizing the significance of this personal connection that she now had with the tooth fairy.

"It's true. When I was a little girl, Nana used to help the tooth fairy out sometimes," I explained. When we were young, my father had a fascination with wiggling our loose teeth. He used to tell us he was helping the tooth fairy keep to her schedule.

"Nani said that Nana always tells the tooth fairy about teeth that fall out of the kids that he knows." I made a mental note—very important to pay attention to every fallen tooth! Nana's reputation was at stake.

I thought about the process of moving from that world of wonder and magic to the world of reality and fact. Children ultimately hear about the nonexistence of the tooth fairy and Santa Claus, and with that information, a bit of magic is taken away from their lives.

How can we as parents continue to foster that sense of wonder, joy, anticipation, and excitement? How can we help our children continue to believe in magic? We reach critical moments in parenting and life where we make choices about how to help our children interpret our world. It's what we do in those moments that fosters their imagination, creativity, hopes, and dreams.

Tara continued her reverie about the tooth fairy—what she looked like, how she got around, what she did with all those teeth. We contemplated writing a personal letter to her, introducing Tara and her teeth, and giving it to Nana to deliver. Tara giggled with excitement as she went to get some paper and crayons, and I continued to think about how to nurture a continuing sense of wonder in my daughter that would feed her imagination for a lifetime.

58

Why can't I stop my body from hitting my little sister?

Tara and Leela were screaming and crying, kicking and hitting each other as they fought. It took me a moment to separate them, and they both continued to cry for a few moments.

"I need you both to settle down," I scolded. "What is going on here?"

Leela, 2 years old, had already been distracted and was playing with some dolls. Tara blurted, "She hit me!"

"Leela, did you hit your sister?" Leela nodded, and then automatically said, "Sowwy, Tawa Didi" and blew her a kiss. Her attention went back to the dolls.

"Why do you think she hit you, Tara?" I asked.

"Well, I took her doll away and then she hit me."

"Sweetie, it's not nice to take other people's things away. You know that."

Tara nodded. "I know, Mama. But even though my mind knew I shouldn't grab the doll, my body still did it."

"Oh!" I could not help but smile. "So your body actually made you grab the toy?" She nodded.

"Well, Tara, you know you always have the power, the choice, to control your body. If your body wants to do something, then you can tell your body to stop."

She was now on a roll. "Mama, I was thinking I should not grab the toy, even while my body did it. I just couldn't stop it!" She was really testing the limits of this explanation.

"Tara, that is not an excuse. I need you to stop your body from doing such things. When your mind tells you something is not right, you can control what happens." She nodded apprehensively.

A month later, we were having a playdate at our house. Six kids under the age of 5 running around, screaming, fighting, crying, laughing—it was utter pandemonium. At night, before we went to bed, Tara confided in me.

"Mom, you know while we were playing, I wanted to join the other kids in throwing all the toys from the chest." I raised my eyebrows.

"My body really wanted to do it, but my mind kept telling me not to. And, you know what, my mind actually stopped my body from doing it!" I could see she felt she had overcome a challenge.

"Tara, I am so proud of you!" I gave her a big hug. "You are a very good girl." She smiled and drifted off to sleep.

Question for Your Child

How does your body feel when you want to laugh?

59

Can I always win?

Tara began to understand the concept of winning and losing when she was around 4 years old. It was fascinating for me to see that my daughter, who had always been a bit shy and reserved, was extremely competitive in the classroom and while playing games with other people. She wanted to be the best and she wanted to win.

When she was playing a game with me, she actually demanded to win. I tried to explain to her that the goal of playing the game was to enjoy the play, not just to win. That, however, did not really seem to address her need for victory. Whenever we have these moments, I wonder how to best foster a healthy competitive drive and balance in my children.

An interaction a few days later during a visit to my parents' house gave me a little insight. My mother wanted Tara to sleep with her in her room, as she looked forward to these visits when she could cuddle with her granddaughter. But now that Tara was mindful enough to make her own decisions, she insisted that she wanted to sleep with me.

I overheard their conversation.

My mom said, "Tara, won't you sleep with me tonight?"

"No, Nani, I want to sleep with Mama."

"But, I really want you to sleep with me..."

Tara pretended to ignore her plea. "Nani, can we watch a movie?"

"Is it okay with your mama?" my mother asked.

"Well, maybe if you tell her I can watch a movie, then we can cuddle in bed and I can sleep with you." I marveled at my daughter's negotiation skills!

"I think that is a great idea!" my mother agreed.

Tara came running to me to tell me that Nani really wanted Tara to watch a movie with her in bed. I gave her a good night hug and told her to have fun.

As Tara was running to her grandmother's room, she turned around and told me, "You know, Mama, Nani and I figured out a way to get what we both really want."

Now that, I thought, is an example of how to create a win-win situation!

Question for Your Child

Is there a way for two people to win a game?

Do I have to be a Muslim?

One day Tara's friend, Aleeha, returned home from school and said to her mother, "Mommy, I want to eat pork." Being from a Muslim family, Aleeha was not supposed to eat pork.

So, her mom's first response was, "Baby, we are Muslim, and Muslims don't eat pork."

Of course, this answer just pushed Aleeha further. "Mommy, then I don't want to be a Muslim anymore. Why can't Muslims eat pork?"

At this point, Aleeha's mother realized that she better be careful how she answered, because Aleeha would hold on to it for months to come. If she told her that Muslims didn't eat pork because historically pigs were considered dirty animals, Aleeha would probably announce in school to all her friends that they were eating dirty animals.

She wondered if Aleeha would understand the concept of tradition, belief, and culture.

"Aleeha, I don't eat pork because my mommy and daddy didn't eat pork. And their mommy and daddy didn't eat pork. Not eating pork is one way of being connected to our family, of being proud that we are Muslim."

"Do I have to be a Muslim? I really want to eat pork."

Her mother took a moment to reflect. So many deeper issues related to this question.

Can we force our children to follow our path? Or do we lead them by example and hope that they will follow? How do we guide them to make decisions that are important to us personally? Is that fair? What does it mean to be Muslim for a 4-year-old girl?

At that moment, Aleeha's mom decided to let Aleeha make her own choice.

"You can eat pork if you want," her mother replied. Aleeha was happy. There was no need to eat it at that moment. And, later that day, Aleeha still joined her mother for the evening prayer.

What Does It Mean to Be Good?

"If you are bad, will you become a dog in
your next life?"

SHYLA (AGE 7)

61

Why do I always have to say thank you?

Tara once asked me why I always make her say thank you—thank you to her teachers after school, thank you to the cleaning lady when she leaves the house, thank you to the waiter who has brought us some food.

"We say thank you to people who help us in our lives," I explained. "We are so lucky to know all these people who make our lives more special. By saying thank you, we show our appreciation."

"And by saying thank you, we show them that we are grateful for everything they do for us."

Tara smiled. She then gave me a big hug.

"Mama, thank you for being my mama and taking me to school and giving me toys and letting me eat ice cream."

"Oh, my *jaan* (life)," I replied with tears in my eyes. "You don't ever have to thank Mama because I am your mama and I love you and want to do everything for you."

"But I want to show you my *preciation* (appreciation)," she said as she hugged me closer.

I agreed. We should also thank each other once in a while.

"Thank you for showing me your appreciation, Darling. I want to thank you for being such a wonderful daughter."

And tickling each other, we both giggled, "Thank you. Thank you. Thank you."

62

Why can't I use that word?

T ara was playing a game on the computer, and I heard her snap, "Oh shit!"

"Hey!" I called over. "We don't use words like that."

"But, Mom," Tara replied, "you use that word sometimes."

"No I don't!" I replied instantly. "I use the word *shoot,* not that word."

"Yes, you do Mama. When there is an utter disaster, you use that word. Why can't I use that word?" I stopped for a moment as I realized that she was right—I probably had used that word—several times, in fact. Tara looked at me with big, wide, challenging eyes.

"You know what, Tara. You are right. I have used that word when there is an utter disaster. But I am sorry. It's not right for me to use that word either."

I wasn't sure if she was buying it.

Words are very powerful, I explained. With our words, we can make people around us feel good or bad. With our words, we show people that we respect them. When we use bad words, then we are not showing respect to those around us.

"Why is shit a bad word?" Tara pushed.

Why is shit a bad word? I asked myself.

"Hmm. Because shit sometimes makes people around us feel bad or sad or angry…" I had to admit I was struggling with this one, so I changed tactics.

"Well, you know what, maybe when it is an utter disaster, sometimes we forget about not using some words. But, most of the time, we should be careful not to use those words if they hurt others."

I continued. "And maybe we should make a deal. I will try not to use that word—even in an utter disaster—if you agree to try not to use that word. Agreed?"

Tara smiled. She got it now. Agreed.

Question for Your Child

What are some words that are okay to use in an utter disaster?

63

Why can't I be perfect?

There is a Chinese fable about two pots. Every day, a villager would walk to the river to fetch water. He carried the water in two pots, each one at the end of a long stick that he carried on his back.

One pot was perfect and would always deliver a full vessel of water. The other pot, however, had a crack on its side. So, by the time the villager reached home, half of the water from the cracked pot had leaked out.

For several years, the villager continued his journey from the river to home, with the perfect and the cracked pot. One day, the cracked pot could not take it anymore.

"Sir, I am miserable because I fail you every day! Why do you not fix my crack so I can be perfect like the other pot?"

The villager smiled at the pot. "Dear pot, you are perfect just the way you are."

The pot did not understand, so the villager continued. "I have always known about your crack, so I planted seeds on your side of the path. Look at these beautiful flowers that you have watered!"

The pot saw the flowers and was proud. Indeed, its crack had created new life and beauty in the world.

64

Why do I have to share?

At 4½, Tara has had some issues with sharing, especially with her little sister who wanted everything that Tara had. As a mom, I had been struggling to figure out how to teach her about sharing, and why it is important. My friend, Grace, showed me the following example. It definitely made an impression on Tara.

"You know why it is important to share?" Grace said to Tara and me.

We both smiled, wondering what she was going to say.

"Tara, can you take this?" Grace handed her a book.

"And this." She handed her another book. "And this and this and this." She handed her a doll, a pen, a pad of paper. Now, more things. A banana, another book, a sweater.

Tara giggled. "I can't hold all these things!" she laughed as several things fell out of her arms.

"Oh, but I wanted to share this necklace with you! Do you want to try this on?" Grace showed her a pretty necklace. Tara's eyes sparkled.

"Well, maybe if you shared some of those things with your mom and your sister, then I could share this necklace with you?" Grace suggested.

Tara handed me the things in her hand, eager to try on the necklace.

"Oh, see now that you shared your things with your mom, you can try on this necklace!" Grace smiled. "Hey, but look at how happy Mom is that she got to see the book you just gave her. Mom, aren't you happy that you got to see that book? Doesn't it make you happy?"

I nodded and smiled.

"See, Tara, when we share things, we make other people happy and we also invite people to share more things with us."

Tara nodded her head. She looked at me and smiled. "It's true, Mama. Sharing is good," she said to me with total seriousness. She got it.

And her attention shifted to the necklace!

Question for Your Child

How does it feel when a friend shares something special with you?

65

Why do I have to forgive her?

Leela at 2 years old was constantly testing her boundaries. And her big sister was most often the object of exploration.

Leela would grab a toy from Tara and scream, "Mine." She would pull her sister's hair. She would hit her. She would try to sit on top of her. Without fail, she would successfully get Tara to react with a cry, a scream, a push, and most often, "Mom, she is bothering me!"

It was generally easy to get Leela to give back the toy or to move. I would look her in the eye and say, "No Leela. Say sorry to Tara." And she would smile and instantly say, "Sowwy Tawa Didi." She would then give her sister a big hug.

The tougher part, however, was getting Tara to accept the apology. Tara would often still be in tears (because her head really hurt from the pull on her hair or she was angry that her toy had been damaged).

"Why do I have to forgive her?" she would ask. "She broke my toy." Or "She hurt me."

It was through these sibling fights that we explored forgiveness.

"Well, if we don't forgive her, Tara, then you will stay hurt and angry. She is ready to love you again, but you will be blocking her love."

"I know, but she keeps hurting me and I didn't do anything!" Tara would justifiably respond.

"She is just testing you, Baby. She loves you most in the world, so she just wants your attention," I explained. "See how sweetly she is hugging you."

At this point, Leela would literally be hanging onto Tara. "Sowwy Tawa Didi! Sowwy Tawa Didi! Sowwy Tawa Didi!" She sounded like a broken record.

Tara could not help but laugh. She hugged her sister back, in part just to get her off of her. "Okay, okay, okay!" she would say, patting her head. "She really is like a little monkey," mature Tara would now say to me.

Appeased, Leela happily moved on to the next activity, and Tara went back to ignoring her until the next time.

66

What are you thankful for?

I was tidying up in our bedroom one morning as Tara and Leela played with each other. Generally their play consisted of 4-year-old Tara telling her 2-year-old sister what to do, while Leela diligently followed the instructions, just so happy to have her big sister's attention.

After a few minutes, I realized it was unusually quiet, so I peeked out from the bedroom door to make sure everything was in order. My two little daughters were both sitting quietly in front of a bronze statue of the Hindu elephant god, Ganesha. Tara's hands were clasped together in prayer, her eyes closed. Leela peeked through her eyes, mimicking her sister's movements.

Tara suddenly proclaimed, "Now sing!" And, the two of them then broke into song, loudly singing an Indian prayer, "Om Jai Jagadish."

After they finished the song, Tara declared, "Be thankful for Diwali." (Diwali is the Indian festival of lights that we had recently celebrated.)

Little Leela repeated, "Be twanful po Dibali."

Then they both put their hands on the ground, obviously mimicking the Muslim prayer they had recently seen Tara's friend offer. They sang "Om Jai Jagadish" again. And Tara said, "Be thankful for India."

Leela repeated, "Be twanful po Indya." And their heads went down again.

I watched them quietly, smiling and so grateful for my precious little girls. They had created their own ritual of expressing gratitude, mimicking notions of a prayer from Manorama, who is Christian, from their little Muslim friend, and from the devotional song, "Om Jai Jagadish," which we learned for Diwali.

Question for Your Child

What are you thankful for?

67

What is kindness?

The parable of the Good Samaritan from the Bible is a nice story about kindness, charity, and compassion.

One day, a man was walking down the road, when some robbers attacked him. They took away all his belongings and hurt him so badly that he could not get up.

As he lay on the ground, a priest, who was supposed to help people, was walking by. The priest, who was late for a meeting, pretended not to see the man, crossed to the other side of the road, and hurried off. The wounded man continued to suffer.

A few minutes later, the wounded man heard footsteps approaching. As he saw the robes of a holy man, he felt relieved and reached out his hands for help. But the holy man backed away from the bloody victim and scurried off.

The wounded man cried and thought he was going to die. Just when he had given up all hope, he felt a man gently wipe the blood from his face and give him some water. He looked up and saw a stranger smiling at him. The stranger helped him get up and walk to a nearby inn. There he cleaned him, fed him food, and helped him get into bed. The stranger gave money to the innkeeper and asked him to take care of the wounded man. The stranger told the innkeeper that if there were any extra expenses, he would take care of them. The important thing was for the man to get better.

And with that, he left. He had taken care of the wounded man with no expectation of thanks or glory, just because it was an act of compassion that came from inside.

68

What is respect?

One day, as Tara was having a tantrum, she shouted at me, "You cannot tell me what to do! I am the boss of myself! You shut your mouth!"

I raised my voice and stated, "Tara, you do not talk to me like that!" Since I am careful to manage my temper with the children, she knew that I was serious. She whimpered off to another room crying. After a bit, I went into the room and asked if she was ready to talk.

"Tara, you need to understand that you cannot speak to Mama or Papa, or anyone for that matter, that way. I do not speak to you that way, do I?" She understood and sincerely said, "Mommy, I am sorry!" She then began to cry, a cry that expressed true regret.

"Sweetie, it's okay." I wiped the tears from her eyes. "But it is important that you always show respect for others."

"But, Mama, what does respect mean?"

I thought for a moment. "Respect is treating other people like we would like to be treated. It is speaking with kindness, being honest and polite, telling the truth, listening, and being fair."

I continued, "And it is important to respect ourselves. When you got so angry just now, it didn't feel good, did it?" Tara nodded her head.

"So you have to respect yourself as well," I said.

As we continued our conversation, I realized that the concept of respect could not be answered just with words. Respect had to be demonstrated every day through our actions and words. I decided that over the next few days, we would pay attention to the ways in which we respected each other and ourselves. We would listen to the words that people used with each other (like *please* and *thank you*), and observe how a smile made someone feel, or how a car stopped to let people cross the street. We would be grateful to people who helped us at home, in a store, or in a restaurant, and we would appreciate all that our teachers at school did for us.

69

Is he naughty or nice?

Sumant and I like to share stories with our daughters. We let them watch limited television and movies, and read them books and comics that tell the stories of classic mythology.

When we opened a new comic book, Tara wanted to know if a character was naughty or nice. Similarly, when we put a movie on, her first question when a new character appeared was if they were naughty or nice. Once she knew, she was able to engage in the narrative in a more relaxed fashion.

I realized that while the stories and characters captivated her imagination, they also portrayed people as either good or bad. I wanted to teach her "goodness," but I also didn't want her to judge people in the world as either good or bad. I was already uncomfortable with this portrayal in the media, and wanted to foster an openness and compassion in my daughters for all people.

One day, as I was dropping her off at school, I opened the car door and a bicyclist swerved to the side. He started screaming at me, and I profusely apologized, admitting I had made a mistake. The man continued to scream and even followed us as I approached her school. Tara clung to me tight, scared. When we got inside the school gates, she asked, "Mama, is he a naughty man?"

I was distraught at his actions, unnerved, and angry, but I also recognized that this was an opportunity to show her that things are not black and white. I explained to her that the man was trying to go for a nice bike ride, and by mistake, I almost hurt him. He was scared, and so he got angry. He probably did not know how to express his anger in any other way but to scream at me.

Tara listened.

"But it's not nice to scream at other people. Mama, he scared me."

"I know you were scared, Sweetie. I was a little bit scared also. But Mama made a mistake and maybe he didn't understand that I was sorry, so he got angry."

I could see her processing the information. "And just because he got angry," I continued, "doesn't mean he isn't a nice man. You and I get angry too sometimes, don't we?" Tara nodded.

I hoped that by explaining the vulnerabilities and hurt and reasons behind choices in those that we perceived to be bad, I could help her (and me) come to terms with so-called bad actions.

70

If God is always watching, why do bad things happen to good people?

A friend of ours was going through a divorce. Her daughter was 4 years old at the time.

The little girl watched her mother struggle and feel betrayed, hurt, and vulnerable. And, even though her mother tried to hide it from her, the little girl saw her mother cry at night when she was supposed to be sleeping.

The little girl had been told that God was always around us. Well, if God was so good, why did he let her mother hurt so much?

I remember thinking the same thing when I was 30 years old, and my 20-year-old cousin was diagnosed with a brain tumor. He lost his sight and hearing and sense of smell due to chemotherapy and radiation. My cousin was a good, energetic, smart, and loving boy.

And most of the people hurt in war or terrorist attacks, like 9/11, are probably good people. Why does God let such things happen?

My friend didn't really know how to answer her 4-year-old's questions. She tried to explain to her daughter that God was a source of strength for Mommy, even though Mommy was hurting. She wanted her daughter to have faith in something larger than herself as a source of power, love, and healing.

I still think about how to talk to Tara and Leela about God in a world that is full of inequality, pain, and suffering.

Do I tell them that when bad things happen to good people, I wonder if God even exists? Is God good?

Do I explain that the universe is made up of dark and light, and we need black to appreciate white?

Do I try to justify that those good people who face bad hurdles get them because in doing so, they can teach us all more about life? Do I really believe that?

Or should I be completely honest with my children and tell them that I really do not know?

I know that when the time comes to answer these difficult questions, I will be honest with them—telling them that I get solace from thinking about God as a source of energy that is love, compassion, and peace. I will hold their hands as they begin their own journeys of exploration about God, hoping that together we will find answers and inspiration.

What's My Purpose?

"What does a rainbow look like
when it dies?"

CLARICE (AGE 6)

71

What kind of work do you do?

One morning, Tara and Leela were sitting at their desk and coloring pictures. Tara asked me, "Mama, what kind of work do you do?"

"Well, I write books, so I guess you can say I am an author." I was always a bit unsure about how to answer this question, as I do not label myself professionally.

Tara continued coloring her picture as she asked, "And what kind of work does Papa do?"

"Papa helps people build their companies." Sumant is a venture capitalist.

"And what about that man you work with? What does he do?" She was having fun with this line of questioning.

I was working on a film. I explained he was a producer and director—he made movies.

"Mama, do you know what kind of work I do?" She looked up from her drawing.

"What kind of work do you do, Tara?" I relented.

She showed me the picture she had been drawing—a heart with Mama, Papa, Tara, and Leela.

She gave me a big smile and said, "I love and protect my family."

What do the goldfish do all day long?

Feeding our new batch of goldfish one morning, Tara asked, "What do the goldfish do all day long?"

Goldfish just exist, I thought. "What do you think they do all day?" I asked.

"Well, they are eating right now." The goldfish were gobbling up a very large handful of fish food that Leela had dropped in for them. "And then they probably will have a nap, go for a swim, and just lie around."

"I wonder if goldfish have feelings?" I said out loud.

"Of course, they do. They are happy now. Look at that one smiling." Tara was able to see the goldfish smile.

"Do you think they ever get bored?" I continued.

She shook her head. She was pretty sure they did not.

"They look up at the sky. They swim. They talk to each other. They eat. They swim behind the rock…" She had begun a list of all the things the goldfish did all day. After a list that went on for several minutes, she finally ended, "They just do their work, whatever they are supposed to do all day long. They live and live."

I smiled and took a deep breath. "Yes, they just live."

Why do you need mommy time?

Being a mother requires wearing many hats. From managing the house, meals, bath time, nap time, and bills, to balancing work and relationships, many days I find very few moments to even sit down. Life with kids gets crazy, and there are times I feel I just can't manage anymore. But then the reality sinks in—as a mom, I can't even let the craziness get to me!

Then there are those days when things are just more difficult. There is a work deadline, no food in the house, the phone doesn't stop ringing, the bills are late, and I have a miserable headache. Inevitably on such days, I find that my daughters, sensing my stress, also demand more attention, fight more, and are generally moody.

My daughters are used to the concept of my needing some mommy time, and my husband respects my need for it. For me, finding some ME time every day has been life transforming. These moments, if tapped into regularly, build up over time to give me a source of peace, perspective, and calmness. Ideally, I can meditate for 15 minutes to catch my breath and be silent. Most often, my mind is racing with all the things I haven't done, forgot to do, or need to do. Nonetheless, I force myself to take the time to decompress. I become more centered, less frantic, and calmer. Family time becomes more focused and more fulfilling.

When my daughters ask me why I need mommy time, the answer is quite simple.

Mommy time makes me a better mommy.

Question for Your Child

When you are alone, what do your thoughts sound like?

74

Why can't I run faster than everyone else?

I admittedly was not a super athlete when I was young. I remember very clearly running in a school race when I was young, and coming in last place. Aside from the fact that I lost the race, I felt humiliated that I was the last one. I felt like everybody would think that I was terrible, that no one would ever choose me for their team, and that my physical impediment would hurt me socially.

I was so somber when I got home that my father asked me what was wrong. I burst into tears and cried about how I could not run fast enough, that everyone was going to make fun of me, and that no one would ever want to play with me again.

My father let me cry and get the emotion out. Then he asked me to articulate what I wanted. "I want to run fast. Faster than everyone else in the class."

"Why do you want to run so fast?" he asked.

"Because I want to win. Because I want people to think I am great and be my friends."

"Mallika, do you like to run?" A simple question that made my tears stop as I thought about it.

"It's okay," I responded, wondering where he was going with this line of questioning.

"What do you really like to do?"

I smiled. "I love to dance."

Now my father had my attention and he spoke. "We all have special talents. Some people can run fast. Some people can sing beautifully. And some people, like you, can dance as effortlessly as the trees sway in the wind."

It was beginning to sink in. Yes, I had my own talents.

"If it is important to you to run fast," my father continued, "then you can decide to focus on running faster. You can train your body to run the best that it can. But you have to decide that it is important for you. Or you can decide to focus on your dancing, which you love."

"And I would guess that when you dance, you are really happy. And when you are really happy, then people will want to be around you." My father gave me a big hug.

I nodded my head. I had to admit that I would rather dance than run. I felt happy when I felt the rhythm of the music in my body, my heart, and my soul. Dancing was my special talent, and I was proud of it.

Question for Your Child

What do you like to do more than anything else?

75

Are we there yet?

It is the question that many parents are used to hearing during a road trip or long flight. Are we there yet? How much longer? When will we get there? At a certain point, after hearing the question a hundred times, we start asking it ourselves! How much longer until we finally get there?

Before a recent road trip, I decided to implement a new strategy *before* getting in the car. With my daughters so young, I felt it was a good time to develop the concept of the journey itself being the destination.

Rather than thinking of our vacation as starting when we reached the hotel, we included packing our bags, driving, getting to the hotel, and settling in our rooms as part of the holiday. It was amazing how this little transition in our minds resulted in a more rewarding overall experience.

Packing our bags became a project that we did together, as we discussed our potential activities during the holiday. We needed bathing suits for the swimming pool, sweaters to wear at night, sneakers for walking around the zoo, and pretty dresses for dinner. We packed our favorite books and dolls and crayons, focusing on the value of each one as we put it in the suitcase. And, most important, we celebrated how much fun we were having packing together.

For the car ride, I made a conscious effort to discuss our surroundings. We looked at the beautiful ocean, noticing the boats, the surfers, the seagulls. Leela, almost 2 years old, was enwrapped in labeling everything we saw, and Tara, the big sister, was sure to tutor her. We sang our favorite songs and told stories. And then we decided to have some quiet time after such a busy afternoon. Their little eyes started to droop, and soon they were asleep. As they slept, my husband and I, who find little time to talk with small kids, actually had some time to catch up.

By the time we reached the hotel, our family had already had a very rich and rewarding time together. And when we remembered the holiday, we always talked about the packing, the drive, and the journey as the special beginning of our holiday together.

76

How can I help others?

Manorama, who helps me take care of Tara and Leela, had hurt her shoulder, and Tara was the first to observe her struggle.

Every morning when Manorama arrived, Tara would ask her how she felt. She would offer to kiss her shoulder to help her feel better and then tell Leela to do the same. (Leela would diligently follow her sister's instructions.)

At the park, Tara would offer to push the swing that Leela was sitting in to make it easier for Manorama. "Manorama, I want to make your life as easy as possible."

And one day she told Manorama, "I love you so much—I don't want you in any pain. How can I take care of you?"

Watching Tara, I realized that as we grow older, we drift away from such genuine compassion and love. Tara's innocence and openhearted empathy for Manorama reminded me that it is our inherent nature to care for and help others.

Question for Your Child

How can you help your friend when he or she is sick?

77

Mommy, am I a good daughter?

Tara and Leela were fighting over some toys, and Tara pushed her little sister. Leela started howling and ran to me to console her.

"She pushed me! Yaya hurt." My 2-year-old was just discovering her ability to string words together and communicate an idea. Tara, realizing she had done something naughty, started to cry, as well. I had two howling little girls pulling at my shirt!

"Tara, did you push your sister?"

Tara nodded. "I'm sorry, Mama!"

"Don't say sorry to me, say sorry to her," I pointed out.

"Sorry Leela." Tara give Leela a hug and a kiss on her curly head of hair. My heart always melted when I saw my two daughters hug each other.

"Sowwy Tawa Didi!" Leela replied. The tears were wiped and things settled down a bit.

"Okay, so what was that all about?" I pushed.

"I wanted that toy and she wouldn't give it to me. And so I hit her, but it was a mistake."

"Tara, you are the big sister. You know you are supposed to take care of Leela and teach her what is good and what is bad. I know you are a good big sister," I asserted.

Tara nodded, and she walked across the room, picked up the toy, and gave it to Leela.

Now she looked at me and asked, "Mama, am I a good daughter, too?"

"My sweetheart. You are a perfect daughter." I hugged her.

"Even if I am naughty sometimes?" she asked, genuinely concerned.

"Tara, you are a good sister, a good daughter, a good granddaughter, a good niece! You love everyone so much and that is what matters," I assured her. "All of us sometimes do things that make people sad, but we can always choose to say sorry and love each other again."

Tara smiled. She walked over to Leela and once again gave her a big hug and kiss and whispered, "Leela, I really love you" into her baby sister's ear.

*Question for Your Child*_____

What makes a good sister or brother?

_____

78

Who are your heroes?

I was reading an early childhood education book that had a section devoted to teaching our children about heroes. It made me think about actively seeking out heroes with Tara and Leela and thinking about their qualities.

So I asked Tara one day if she knew what a hero was. Not really, she replied.

I explained to her that a hero was a person who was brave and kind and helped others.

"Is Mulan a hero?" Somehow in our house, Disney princesses always crept back into our dialogue.

"Yes, Mulan is a hero because she helped her family and the people in China. And she was very brave and true to who she wanted to be." In my further exploration of teaching children about heroes, I had read that children will often refer to pop stars or popular media characters as heroes, and that rather than negate them as heroes, a better strategy would be to point out the characteristics that children could emulate.

"Let's think of other people who could be heroes," I suggested.

"Well, maybe my Nani (grandmother) is a hero, because she takes care of me and you."

I smiled. "Yes, Nani is definitely one of my heroes. In fact, she takes care of her whole family—her children, her husband, her sisters and parents, cousins, nephews, and nieces."

"Yes, Nani is really good," Tara affirmed again.

"And is Candi Mami a hero?" Tara asked. Candi Mami (Candice) is my brother's wife and an eye surgeon. The night before, Candice had come home from the hospital and told us about a surgery she had done that saved a child's eyesight. Tara had listened intently.

"Candi Mami is definitely a hero."

"Mommy, I want to be a hero, too," Tara smiled.

"Sweetie, to me you are a hero because you make me happy!" I continued. "But let's keep our eyes out for other heroes in our world, because then we will really know how to be one."

Tara jumped up, excited, ready to search for some heroes.

Question for Your Child

Who are *your* heroes?

79

When do I have to get a job?

Tara loved to imagine the various things she could do when she grew up. A nanny, dancer, astronaut, architect, hairdresser, mailwoman, and dog doctor were just a few professions on her list. She then went through a phase where she was pretty consistent about becoming a doctor, a teacher, and a mom.

One day, she asked me, "But mom, when can I start working? When do I have to get a job?" It seemed like a simple question, but as I opened my mouth, I was actually at a loss for words. I realized getting a job, working, and doing what you really want are not necessarily aligned for all people. How could I help steer my daughter to make her work her play?

"Tara, many people get a job to earn money so that they can live in a home, buy food and clothes, and take care of people that they love," I began. "But, since you are so young, you don't have to worry about that now because your mama and papa take care of you."

"But," I continued, "I see that you are always working."

"I am?" She was confused.

"Yes, you work on your letters and numbers, and you help me clean up the toys. You clean the table for me sometimes. You comb your dolls' hair and wash their clothes. You make cards for people on their birthdays. Oh, and you cook dinner sometimes in your play kitchen."

She laughed. "But, Mom, all those things are playing, not working!"

Tara, that is the secret, I thought. Think of your work as play.

"I know, but that is what the best work is—play! If we are doing something that makes us happy and smile, then we will be good at it."

Tara paused for a moment. "Well, I am really good at playing with my baby sister and teaching her how to play games. So I guess I don't have to wait to be a teacher!"

Question for Your Child

What do you want to do when you grow up?

80

How do you sing your songs?

Our family was in the car when Tara burst out into song. Sumant and I looked at each other in shock. She was singing the lyrics of a popular song from the radio in perfect tune. And not only was she singing beautifully, she was using her voice to give it her own unique sound.

Sumant and I listened quietly as she proceeded to sing the chorus and then hum, "Ahh Haa Haa. Ahh Haa Haa..." We did not want to make her self-conscious, so when she was done, we remained silent.

Over the next few days, I noticed Tara was humming more songs to herself, many of which were Bollywood songs with lyrics she did not even understand. As someone who cannot carry a tune myself, I was baffled at Tara's talents—they obviously did not come from me! I credited Manorama, who watches and teaches my children while I work, with exposing them to melody. She spent a lot of time singing with them, and Tara had probably heard the pop song with her.

Finally, after a week of listening to Tara's songs, I asked her, "Sweetie, you sing so unbelievably well. How did you learn to sing like that?"

Tara replied, "Mom, the songs just come from inside of me."

Effortless, spontaneous, and innocent. It was such a simple and pure truth.

What Is Love?

"When is our dog coming
back from heaven?"

LOGAN (AGE 4)

81

Where did I come from?

My little baby, you came from a place of love—a place of joy, compassion, and tenderness.

You came from the silent, most intimate spaces between thoughts—that place where all hope and inspiration come from. You came from the place where dreams are made, where blessings are given, where gifts are bestowed.

You came from the earth which feeds and nourishes you, and from the sun which sheds its divine light on you. You came to me from the winds and the rains, from the stars and the moon. You came to me singing praises of the universe which is your home.

Your little cry echoed the voices and spirits of all those that came before you—those that celebrated and cheered when they knew that you were in my arms. You came with a familiar look in your eyes, a smile that I had seen before, a soul that I had already loved forever.

My little baby, you came from the place that brings tears and laughter, which hums the songs of your soul, which dances to the rhythms of a greater spirit.

You came from the place that sings eternally of love.

82

Can you kiss my boo-boo?

There is something magical about Mama's kiss when Baby gets a boo-boo. The kiss seems to take the pain away, almost instantaneously. The kiss settles down the sobs and slows down the tears.

Sometimes it takes several kisses to find the exact location of the boo-boo. If Baby hurts the top of her pinky, Mama may kiss the hand at first. But Baby points to the boo-boo again. So Mama then kisses the fingers, but again, Baby has to show where the boo-boo really is. Finally, Mama kisses the top left side of the pinky. She kisses and kisses it to make sure that the boo-boo has really been taken care of.

Sometimes it takes days of kissing the boo-boo before it feels better. Even after the Band-Aids are gone, Baby will suddenly remember the boo-boo and show it to Mama. Mama really can't see it anymore, but she will kiss it nonetheless.

And Baby will also be kind to Mama's boo-boos. When Mama gets hurt, Baby will want to kiss Mama's boo-boos over and over again. Baby wants to take care of Mama and not let her hurt.

Kissing boo-boos is special Mama-Baby time. Mama will always cherish kissing those sweet little boo-boos.

83

Why do you have to leave me?

When she was 2 years old, saying good-bye to Leela could be a heart-wrenching process. She sensed that I was getting ready to leave the house and would become extra clingy. She would hold me tight, as if by grasping on to me, I would not have the heart to actually leave her.

And then would come the crying, the tears, and the pleading "Mama, no go!" Her little heart breaking as she held onto my leg as I tried to walk out the door.

"Oh, Baby! Mama is just going out for a little while. I will be back soon," I would tell her, trying not to let my voice give away my aching heart. I would hug her and wipe away her tears. I would look her in the eyes and say, "Mama loves you. I promise I will be back soon." Even though the routine had played itself out so many times before, it was just as difficult.

Did I really have to go out right now? Should I stay behind? Would she feel like I was abandoning her for real? Was she thinking, "Why does Mama have to leave me?" I wanted her to feel like Mama is always there for her. I wanted to build up her confidence and her trust that Mama would always come back—by leaving and coming back, I hoped that she was learning that I would always come back for her. But in that moment when she clung onto my legs, my emotions betrayed logic and my heart broke thinking she felt I was leaving her.

Finally, I would lunge out of the house, the high-pitched screams still bellowing in the background. Standing outside the door, I would wait for a moment, hoping the cries would end soon.

And, invariably, the cries did stop. In a few moments, she was distracted and engaged in a new activity. Her attention diverted for a while. And, every once in a while, when she remembered that I had gone, she would point to the door and ask, "Mama?"

When I would come home, she would come running, smiling, and happy that I was back. A big hug, kisses all over. And I would say, "Mama is back! Mama always comes back! Mama loves loves loves you!" I would hold her tight, telling her from my soul that Mama would never really leave her.

Question for Your Child

How does it feel when Mama comes back?

84

Can a flower girl get married?

My cousin asked Tara to be a flower girl at her wedding. Tara did not know what a flower girl was, but the combination of the words *flower* and *wedding* in the same sentence definitely got her excited.

When my cousin explained to her that she wanted Tara to dress up in a pink and gold lehnga (traditional Indian skirt and blouse) and spread rose petals along a path, Tara was instantly taken to a fantasyland of pretty princesses. Really, life could not get any better.

For the next week, Tara incessantly asked questions about the wedding, the bride, flower girl duties, the dress, and the rose petals. As pink was her favorite color, she fantasized about what shade of pink the dress would be and how much gold would actually be on the dress—the shinier the better.

"Can a flower girl get married?" Tara asked one afternoon.

It was amazing to me that at 4½ years old, Tara already had concepts of romance and marriage. She loved to look at our wedding photos. She loved the happily-ever-after endings of fairytales. One day, we entered a hotel at the same time as a bride, dressed in her white wedding dress with long veil. Tara was literally speechless and in awe.

"Of course, flower girls can get married. But when they get married, they will have their own weddings."

"But I want to get married when I am a flower girl."

"Hmm. But who will you marry?" I asked.

Her eyes sparkled, almost mischievously. "Well, I will have to find a boy. And then I will have children. And I will live in my own house."

Yes, you will probably one day find someone to marry. And a wave of emotion overtook me. One day my baby girl would be a woman. I was nostalgic already for this moment.

"But even if you are married, you will always be my little girl. Forever and for always." I held my little flower girl tightly in my arms, savoring her warmth, her smell, and her very touch.

Question for Your Child

Will you still be my baby when you get married?

85

How much do you love me?

I could see from the first moment that my mother held Tara that a floodgate of love had been unleashed. It was a love that was so pure and warm and all encompassing. My mother could not stop smiling, and becoming a grandmother gave her strength and power.

When my mother held Leela, my second daughter, I saw that the love only grew exponentially more. There was no division, no less love for anyone else. Just more love, more kisses, more hugs, more smiles.

My mother's favorite cuddling game with my daughters is to hold them in her lap and kiss every part of their bodies. "I love your toes. I love your tummy. I love your nose. I love your lips. I love your eyes. I love you. I love you. I love you."

And my kids laugh with glee, relishing each kiss, each tickle, and each hug. One more kiss only adds more happiness and more security.

My mom then ends with, "I love you more than the sun, more than the moon, more than the stars, more than the whole wide world!"

And the girls reach their hands out as wide as they can and say, "Nani, I love you this much and even more and more and more!"

Do you love yourself?

My friend, Susie, was sitting with her two children eating ice cream. Her 3-year-old son, Ely, said, "Mommy, I love ice cream!"

Her 2-year-old daughter, Everly, then piped in, "Me love gray cat." This was the cute gray cat that lived next door.

And so began a game of singing out what each one loved.

Susie pointed to both her laughing children and said, "Mommy loves Ely and Everly very much!"

And Ely pointed his little finger back at his mom and asked, "But, Mommy, do you love yourself?"

Question for Your Child

What do you love about yourself?

87

How did you choose me as your baby?

I went into a place deep inside myself where all things are possible. I was quiet and I asked for the most beautiful baby in the world.

I asked for a baby whose smile would brighten up the universe, whose eyes would sparkle like the stars, and whose voice would sound like divine music.

I asked for a baby whom I could hug and kiss 1,000 times every minute.

I asked for a baby whose cries would make me feel deeper than I ever felt before and whose giggles would stir my heart with utter, infinite joy.

I asked for a baby whose soul was gentle and wise and playful.

I imagined your face, your fingers and toes, your legs and arms, your eyes, your little nose and lips. I imagined your little heart beating. And I could smell your baby smell and feel your baby warmth as I asked for you, my little darling.

I asked for you to come into my world so that I could play and laugh and cry and love you forever and forever.

88

Do you like my present?

It was Tara's friend's seventh birthday. Her mother decided to bring her over for a playdate before going for their family celebration dinner.

When the doorbell rang, I casually said, "Oh, Tara. It's too bad we didn't get Pria a birthday present for today." I went to open the door.

As Pria and her mother entered the house, I gave Pria a hug and wished her, "Happy Birthday!" I turned around and couldn't see 4½-year-old Tara.

Tara came running from inside her room. She was holding two bags. She smiled and handed them to Pria. "Happy Birthday, Pria!"

Tara had sweetly run to her room while I had gone to open the door, and put a pair of her shoes in one bag and one of her shawls in another bag. Since we had not bought a present for Pria, she had decided to give her some of her own things.

I watched how happy and excited Tara was to give these gifts to her friend. It did not matter that the shoes were too small for Pria. The important thing was that the gifts had truly come from the heart, from a place of genuine friendship and love.

89

Will you love me even if I am bad?

We were sitting on an airplane, and Tara was tipping a cup full of apple juice with a straw. It was an accident waiting to happen, and I told her to stop because if it spilled, she would be wet for the whole flight.

She ignored me and continued her game. Five seconds later, the cup spilled all over her. She was sopping wet and sticky. Her immediate reaction was to look at me with her big eyes, knowing that I would be upset.

"See Tara. I told you that would happen! Why don't you listen to me?" I scolded.

I focused on wiping the puddle of juice in her lap and the sticky liquid that ran down her leg. "I told you not to do that…" I murmured to myself, completely engrossed in wiping her down.

Tara was completely silent.

When I was done, I finally looked at her face. She was holding back big tears in her eyes. "I'm so sorry, Mama." The tears always got to me.

"It's okay, Baby," I relented. "But we have no change of clothes, so you are going to have to be wet for the rest of the plane ride…"

She nodded her head, accepting the reality of her wet, sticky clothes. She sat quietly as I flipped through a magazine.

About 10 minutes later, she quietly asked, "Mommy, do you still love me?" The question hung in the air. Totally innocent, pure, and vulnerable.

My heart broke. She had been silently crying inside.

"Oh, my love!" I turned to her. "Of course, I love you. Oh, I love you so much!"

"Even if I am bad…?" she asked.

"Sweetheart, I will always love you. No matter what. No matter what you do or say or think or act." I wiped away a tear that had begun to fall.

"You know, sometimes, Mama gets sad and frustrated if you don't listen to me or if you are naughty. But that never means that I don't love you. Always remember that, okay?"

"Okay," she responded.

"Do you think you could sit in my lap for a few minutes?" I asked.

"But I am all wet and sticky…" she admitted.

"I think it is okay if I get a little bit wet and sticky if I can get a hug and a kiss from my daughter." I smiled.

Tara jumped out of her seat and into my lap, giving me one of the warmest, more relieved, and strongest hugs she had ever given me.

90

Does the Earth love me?

Just like I am your mother and love and care for you, the earth is our Mother.

She is your mother, my mother, my mother's mother, and the mother to every person, every animal, every tree, and every drop of water.

So just as you love me, and I love you, Mother Earth loves you too. She gives us sun to keep us warm, rain to quench our thirst, and the earth to grow our food. She gives to us from her body and from her soul. She gives her love to us over and over again.

But, just as Mother Earth loves, she also feels pain and sorrow and joy and hope. If we hurt Mother Earth, she cries. And it gets harder for her to keep giving us all her gifts and her love.

So, even though Mother Earth will love us for eternity, let us not take her love for granted.

Let us show her our love for her over and over again, just as she shows us her love for us.

Question for Your Child

How can we show the Earth that we love her?

Where Is My Soul?

"Mommy, is the sound of God the air?"

BENNY (AGE 4)

91

Where do my stories come from?

Every evening before we sleep, we cuddle in bed and read books. Generally, a set of four books will last a week, and we read all of them every night before rotating to the next set. I notice that during the day, Tara will pick up the same books and retell the story from memory, and Leela will point to the pictures identifying objects like Bow Wow (dog), Moon, and Bunny.

Sometimes, we change our routine a bit. Instead of reading a book, I bring a piece of paper and a pen, and Tara recites a story to me. Her stories capture bits and pieces of the hundreds of stories she has heard, but each one has its own bit of creativity and color. She loves to give her characters original names and loves to explore relationships—between a mama and her daughters, a dog and its owner, a girl and her friends. Often, I can sense from her stories that she is processing an event or interaction from the day. She repeats things I have said to her, and tests out words and phrases whose meaning she does not necessarily understand. After she recites the story, I read it back to her. She listens carefully, letting the story sink in. And usually the next morning, she wants me to read it to her again.

One day, after Tara told a particularly creative story, I asked her, "Where do your stories come from?" She closed her eyes for a moment and said, "From my heart, Mama."

It was such an honest and beautiful answer, and it had a strong impact on me. Her response made me think about how in our life stories, we often drift from the heart to the head. We try to make sense of our worlds, rationalizing, editing, and trying to rewrite over and over again. Listening to Tara's stories has helped me reconnect with my pure, heartfelt voice.

Question for Your Child

How do you think up your stories?

92

Do I have to brush my teeth after I die?

Tara's preschool had a pet spider. One day when the children went to look at the spider, it would not move. The spider had died. The teachers and children decided to bury the spider, and each child wrote a letter to the spider.

I smiled as I read the letters that had been posted on the wall—a common theme emerged from the letters. The children wanted the spider to remember to brush his teeth.

For the children, the spider had moved to another sphere, another world, where it still could make choices, was cognizant, and was active. Even after the spider had been buried, they felt in their hearts that he was still present.

What a lovely way to contemplate and accept death. Thinking about ones I loved and had lost, I imagined their souls laughing as they eavesdropped on my visions of them brushing their teeth in the afterlife.

93

Why do you pray?

Sitting in bed one morning next to Tara as she was waking up, I meditated. When I opened my eyes, I saw Tara thoughtfully watching me.

"Mama, who are you praying to?"

I was quiet for a few moments. I told her to close her eyes. I told her to feel her breath. Could she hear her heart? Could she feel my love for her?

I peeked and saw her seriously nodding her head, her eyes tightly closed.

Well, that love is not only me loving you, but the universe loving you. It's my love, Papa's love, and Leela's love. And the love of everyone in the whole wide world combined. I closed my eyes again.

When we pray, we tell the universe and everyone that loves us that we love them too. And we promise each other to take care of each other forever and ever!

She took my hand. And we sat together for a few more moments, our eyes closed, praying together.

Question for Your Child

Is there something you pray for every day?

94

Can I always stay awake?

We were in the car, when a song we had recently heard at a Bollywood concert came on. Tara smiled. "Remember, Mama, how we heard this song? Leela, do you remember?"

I glanced back and took in the joy of Tara's expression. Her eyes were wide with excitement, sparkling with anticipation for the song.

"Tara, I don't think Leela remembers the song from the concert, because she was sleeping by the time they performed it," I commented.

"Mom," Tara began, her tone sounding almost exasperated, "just because she was sleeping doesn't mean her ears weren't open! Right, Leela?"

Two-year-old Leela nodded her head, enthusiastically agreeing with whatever her big sister said. Leela danced, and as Tara's head bobbed, I knew that she was indeed remembering the song. Once again, my daughters reminded me what it means to be present in each moment, whether we are awake or asleep.

Question for Your Child

What happens to your thoughts when you are sleeping?

95

How is your soul feeling today?

One evening, we found one of Tara's new goldfish dead in the pond. Tara took it in stride, but before going to bed, she began asking questions about where the goldfish had gone.

I explained to her that the soul of the goldfish had left its body. So, while the goldfish was dead—not with us in our life anymore—its soul had floated away and was still alive.

"So, actually, only its body is dead?" she asked.

"Yes, that's how I think of it," I answered. "Souls choose which bodies they **want to** live in for a while. When they are ready to move on, they leave the body."

"Where do they go? Can we see them?" She was fascinated.

"Well, we can't see them, but we can feel them," I answered.

"Really! How?" she asked excitedly.

"Close your eyes and let's be quiet for a moment."

We both sat silent in the bed. Tara naturally put her hands together in a praying position.

"Can you feel your soul, how it is listening to my words?"

Tara enthusiastically nodded her head, her hands still in prayer and her eyes squeezed really tight.

"Your soul and my soul are both connected. We will always be connected."

"Mom, I think I can feel the goldfish's soul…" she dreamily said.

"Really?" I quietly said.

"Yes. My soul is telling its soul to be happy."

And, with that, she opened her eyes, laid down, and drifted off to sleep.

Question for Your Child

Can our souls talk to each other without words?

Have we met before?

My brother woke up early one morning and crawled into bed with my parents. He was about 7 years old.

"Papa, I had a dream last night about you and me."

My dad, just waking up, picked up Gotham and put him in his lap.

"You and I were on a bridge in China. I think we were friends, although we could have been brothers."

My dad listened intently, letting Gotham tell his story.

"We were sitting cross-legged, not talking. Just being with each other, sharing a bowl of rice. It was a beautiful, peaceful day. We were happy."

My father and Gotham sat together in the bed. Quiet, peaceful, and happy.

Question for Your Child

Do you think we knew each other before you were born?

97

Where does God live?

My friend, Suzanne, took her son Hunter to church one morning. Hunter, excited, talked animatedly to his mother. The pastor, who was giving his sermon seriously, was annoyed at the little boy's chatter.

She whispered, "Hunter, please be respectful; you are in God's house."

Hunter looked around him, laughed loudly, and said, "God's house! Where is God's bedroom? I don't see any bedrooms or even a kitchen here!" His words echoed in the church.

The pastor had been once again interrupted and wasn't at all happy about it.

"Shhh," Suzanne said, "you have to keep your voice down." She smiled at the pastor, who returned a grave stare. But Hunter had more questions.

"What, is he taking a nap or something? Is that why I can't see his bedroom? Can I go in after he wakes up?" A few giggles erupted from the congregation.

Suzanne quietly explained that God was not a person the way Hunter was imagining him. She suggested that he think of God as a feeling, a being, that is everywhere and in everything.

Without missing a beat, Hunter replied, "Well, if God is everywhere, then I don't have to be quiet at all, because he must have certainly heard me be loud before!"

98

Where is heaven?

Tara's friend, Kyle, wanted to learn more about heaven. His mother explained to him that heaven is a place where good people go.

Kyle was quiet for a few minutes.

"Mom," he began, "are we bad people?"

"No, Sweetie, why do you think that?" she replied.

Kyle innocently continued, "Well, if we are good, why do we live in Los Angeles and not in heaven?"

With that, his mom explained that heaven was a place where we good people go when the time is right. And that Kyle, with his good heart and kind spirit, would definitely be there one day.

Why is her god a man,
and mine is an elephant?

My niece, Ambika, asked her father why her nanny's god was a man (her nanny was Catholic) and why her god was an elephant (the Hindu god, Ganesha). Similarly, Tara was fascinated by the fact that her friend at school prayed to Jesus, Aleeha (another friend) prayed to Allah, and Tara prayed to lots of different gods.

"Actually everyone is praying to God, we all just choose to see him or her in different ways," I explained.

"God isn't a girl," Tara laughed.

"Why not?" I questioned. "We pray to Parvati (Goddess of Wealth) and Saraswati (Goddess of Wisdom)."

I had a flashback to an encounter with one of my closest friends from college—a born-again Christian—who had told me that since I didn't pray to Jesus, I was a sinner. I thought about how most wars were fought in the name of God. How could we collectively create a different paradigm of thinking for our children?

"You know, the beauty of knowing God lies in the many ways we can discover him or her," I explained. "We can feel God in a church."

"Like when those people were singing?" I had taken Tara and Leela to a gospel service a few weeks earlier, and they both were mesmerized.

"And remember when we went to the temple in India with your great-grandfather?" Tara nodded. At the temple, there were many gods dressed in extravagant clothes.

Now Tara piped in. "Mama, Aleeha prays with her mama every day."

"So, the important thing for us to remember, my love, is that it does not really matter how we speak to God, just that we feel comfortable with God. God is with us all the time in spirit."

Tara thought for a few moments. "Mama, I really liked that singing. Can we go to the church again?"

It was an unexpected request—after all, our family identified ourselves as Hindus, not churchgoers. But, listening to my heart and the words we had just uttered echoing in my ears, I agreed. After all, ultimately I wanted to cultivate for Tara and Leela a relationship with spirit that would stay with them throughout their lifetimes.

100

When will I meet God?

By the age of 1, both of my daughters would put their hands together whenever they saw a statue or painting of a god. "Jai," they would say, mimicking the traditional Indian gesture of respect. With smiles on their faces, they would glance at whoever was watching to note how it made them happy.

Tara's favorite stories were mythological ones, and she loved to imagine the adventures of gods and goddesses from different traditions. She listened intently to stories of Jesus Christ and the Buddha.

When we visited India, we went to temples, mosques, and gurdwaras. And I liked to take the girls to church services with gospel music. Personally, I felt such exposure to all religions would give them a sense of the divine.

One day, Tara asked me, "Mama, when will I actually meet God?"

Looking at her, I sensed that her question was very earnest. I took a moment to think about how I should respond.

"Well, we meet God all the time."

"We do?" she responded.

"Sit here." I smiled and tapped the sofa next to me. Tara skipped happily to sit beside me—she loved these conversations.

I got up and put some music on—Sufi devotional music by Nusrat Fateh Ali Khan. Tara loved this music.

"Do you feel joy in your heart?" I whispered. She smiled, and together we listened to the song.

"Every time we feel joy in our hearts, it is God reminding us that he loves us. Sometimes he comes when we pray, other times when we look at something beautiful, or maybe even when we are playing and laughing," I explained.

"So, we meet God with our feelings, and not for real?" Tara questioned.

I smiled. "Yes, God is everywhere around us. And whenever you want to meet him, you just need to feel him and he will be there."

She nodded. And I knew deep down inside that she understood.